First Edition

Eye of the Storm
Essays in the Aftermath

Ellen Wood Rickert
Editor

Coastal
Carolina Press

Wilmington, North Carolina

Eye of the Storm: Essays in the Aftermath
Edited by Ellen Wood Rickert

 Coastal
Carolina Press

Coastal Carolina Press
4709 College Acres Drive, Suite 1
Wilmington, NC 28403 U.S.A.
www.coastalcarolinapress.org

First Edition, 2000

Book designed by Maximum Design, Inc.

Printed in the United States of America
Applied for Library of Congress Cataloging - in - Publication Data

ISBN 1-928556-12-4

Printed on recycled paper.

Eye of the Storm: Essays in the Aftermath
This book is dedicated to those—human and otherwise—who lost their lives and homes, and to those who risked their own lives to save others, throughout the 1999 storm season.

Acknowledgments

I would like to personally thank all of our contributors, who gave generously of their time and talents in sharing their experiences, thoughts, and expertise. Each of the essays lends a different perspective to the collective work. To all of you, I am grateful.

Many thanks to everyone at Coastal Carolina Press: Emily Colin and Tony Norris for coming in early, staying late, and showing up on their days off when the deadline for the book loomed; Chris Compton and Dorothy Gallagher for holding up the business end of things; and Andy Scott, our Director and the man with the twenty-first century vision–thank you for allowing me to pursue this project and see it through to its fruition.

To Amy Tharrington and Kelly Carter at Maximum Design, who understood the vision I had for the book and made it one we can all be proud of—you're awesome.

For Wilmington's wonderful women and the folks at the kitchen, I couldn't have done it without you all. Of course I have to thank Brian, my husband of over twenty years for his unending patience, and my children, Jessica and Christopher, for their inspiration.

And last, but certainly not least, I thank God for keeping all of us safe and healthy during the storms.

TABLE OF CONTENTS

Part I: Hurricanes

Part II: Environmental Impact

Part III: People in Peril

Part V: What Next? Life on the Edge

Part I Hurricanes

Hurricanes: The Way of the Winds

By

George Elliott

Humans get in the way. We inhabit a planet that can be tranquil as a baby's breath or as violent as a raging inferno. Vast forest fires, volcanoes, and the hurtling winds of hurricanes are the natural consequences of life in a turbulent universe. Hurricanes have always been a part of Earth's history, and will likely always be a part of its future. We can't stop them, nor, given today's human knowledge and abilities, alter them in any way. Our only hope is to better forecast and prepare for them.

The word hurricane comes from the colonial Spanish and Caribbean Indian words for "evil spirits" and "big winds." Storms west of the international dateline are called "typhoons." In the Southern Hemisphere they are referred to as "cyclones." However, it is not what they are called that matters—it is what they do.

There is a very good reason, at least as far as the Earth's atmosphere is concerned, that these monster storms form in the first place. Our planet is sphere-shaped, angled at some 23 $^1/_3$ degrees to the plane of the sun, and has a surface whose nature varies from dark soils to rock formations to water. Thus, it is heated unequally. Our weather patterns continually equalize temperature and moisture distribution over the globe.

Hurricanes efficiently transport excess heat and moisture from the tropics to the poles. They start out as a cluster of showers and thunderstorms surrounding an area of relatively low pressure. Given water temperatures of 80 degrees Fahrenheit or higher, and favorable upper-air weather patterns (high pressure and light winds well up into the atmosphere), these harmless rain squalls can grow into immense "heat engines" in a matter of days.

By some estimates, larger hurricanes stir up over a million cubic miles of the atmosphere every second. The biggest storms can also process 20 billion tons of water each day, and their top wind speeds occasionally reach 300 miles per hour. Meteorologists estimate that strong storms daily produce energy equivalent to the simultaneous explosion of hundreds of atomic bombs. Throughout the course of its life cycle, a single hurricane produces enough energy to satisfy the world's needs for several years.

Of course, hurricanes come in a variety of sizes and intensities. The Saffir-Simpson scale is used to attach a number, or category, to hurricanes. The scale ranges from category one, the weakest, with wind speeds under 96 miles per hour, to category five, where wind speeds exceed 155 miles per hour. The scale was named after two gentlemen who established the scale in the early 1970s: Herbert Saffir, a consulting engineer, and Robert Simpson, then the director of the National Hurricane Center.

As alluded to earlier, for hurricanes to grow, they have to form over vast stretches of open water. Sea surface temperatures must be 80 degrees Fahrenheit or higher where rain squalls are gathering around an area of relatively low pressure near the surface of the earth. Winds blow inward toward low pressure, thus forcing the colliding air currents to rise. These rising warm and moisture-laden air currents foster the rain squalls' growth. Additionally, and coincident with these warm waters and surface low pressure, winds in the upper atmosphere must be light. Strong upper-level winds would blow apart the developing rain squalls and thunderstorms. This process is known as "shearing." In other words, strong winds literally "shear" apart the environment in which a hurricane may be trying to form.

If the environment to this point is conducive to development, one more condition must exist in order for a hurricane to successfully form. Air must be evacuated from the top of these rising currents of heat and moisture. This is accomplished by the presence of high pressure in the upper atmosphere. In the areas of high pressure, winds blow outward from the center. This process, if situated over a developing hurricane, acts as a chimney to remove the heat that's rising into the upper atmosphere from below. This keeps the hurricane from choking itself to death, and permits continuation of the lower-level inflow of warm and moist air.

These conditions increase in frequency during June and July, and persist into November. However, the peak of hurricane season is mid-September, with the vast majority of storms forming during August and September. Within these months, the frequency of hurricane formation shifts from the Gulf of Mexico and Caribbean in June and July to the Atlantic Ocean in August and September, then back to the Caribbean and Gulf during October and November.

We all know how destructive hurricanes can be. Ordinary objects can be transformed into lethal projectiles when driven by powerful winds. These winds are rendered even more destructive when they whip heavy rain sideways. The storm surge, a rolling and building tidal wave of water above normal tide levels, causes the most damage to coastlines and barrier islands. Where the undersea shelf slopes gently, as is the case along the Carolina shores, the storm surge can literally tear away huge portions of beaches and anything on them. The surge can also flood low-lying areas farther inland. Heavy rains can quickly saturate millions of acres, causing extensive and long-lasting flooding. In addition, as the hurricane makes landfall, tornadoes are frequently spawned in the heavy rainbands that accompany the storm.

Not terribly long ago, meteorologists could obtain little, if any, knowledge that a hurricane was about to strike. The famous Galveston, Texas storm of 1900 killed thousands, mainly because meteorologists were unable to predict a massive storm surge that was about to impact the area. Hurricane forecasting did not become much more accurate until the advent of satellite technology in the 1960s. Today, scientists possess sophisticated weather-sensing equipment, as well as more information about the genesis of these massive storms. There is a long way to go, but progress continues.

Hurricanes will always be a part of life on earth. For those who choose to live in areas frequently in the "eye of the storm," a healthy dose of respect for these storms' awesome power is well advised.

George Elliott

George Elliott began his career as chief meteorologist at WZZM in Kalamazoo, Michigan. He has also served as on-camera meteorologist at The Weather Channel and CNN graphics meteorologist. Currently, George works as chief meteorologist at WECT-TV in Wilmington, North Carolina. He has published a weather forecasting book, *Weather Forecasting, Rules, Techniques and Procedures*, and his forecasts have the AMS (American Meteorological Society) and NWA (National Weather Association) "Broadcast Seal of Approval."

Hurricane Floyd: North Carolina's Greatest Storm?

As much of eastern North Carolina begins the long and grueling process of drying out and recovering from the record flooding left by Hurricane Floyd, many are already calling the storm the worst in the state's history. When compared with other hurricanes of the past, Floyd appears to be a good candidate for that notorious title.

"Though other hurricanes have landed with more ferocious winds and tides, Floyd's copious rains and the resulting floods have created a disaster unlike any our state has seen," said Jay Barnes, author of *North Carolina's Hurricane History* (UNC Press). "Though the death toll may climb higher and the dollar damages are still being tallied, we can already see that Floyd will be remembered as North Carolina's worst hurricane," Barnes said.

When Floyd made landfall near Cape Fear last week, maximum sustained winds were estimated at 110 mph, making the hurricane a strong category two on the Saffir-Simpson scale. Many other hurricanes have struck the state with greater intensity, including Hurricane Fran in 1996, which was a category three.

Hurricane Hazel, which swept inland over Brunswick County in October 1954, was the benchmark storm for an entire generation of Tar Heel residents. Its 140 mph winds and 17 ft. storm surge place it among a rare group of hurricanes—the only category four to make landfall in North Carolina in the twentieth century. No category five has ever hit the state, according to Barnes' research.

Though Floyd will not be remembered as the most intense, it is already among the most deadly of the state's natural disasters. Only one hurricane has killed more people in the state's history. In September 1883, a violent storm killed 53 people along the Cape Fear River near Wilmington. Hurricane Hazel was responsible for 19 deaths in the state, Fran killed 24. At least 40 deaths were blamed on the August 1879 hurricane that struck Carteret County, and the San Ciriaco Hurricane of August 1899 killed 25.

State and federal officials will be busy for weeks compiling the total dollar losses left in

Floyd's wake. Early estimates suggest that the agricultural destruction alone may top $1 billion.

Across the eastern third of the state, officials concede that the total losses could easily surpass the $5.2 billion estimate placed on Fran. In contrast, Hurricane Hazel's toll was a mere $136 million.

"We clearly have entered the era of billion-dollar hurricanes in North Carolina," Barnes said Friday. "The storms of the fifties have been wholly eclipsed by Fran and Floyd, largely because of the extensive growth that has occurred in the state."

North Carolina is Hurricane Alley: A Historical Perspective

By

Jay Barnes

"Oh no, not another one!" exclaimed the Wilmington radio announcer as he read the latest wire report with disbelief. "Not another one. We can't stand another big storm." But it was true. Another powerful hurricane was spinning toward the Tar Heel coast, the third to threaten the region within the past few weeks. The first two had already pounded several eastern counties, and this one was also destined to strike, perhaps a little farther up the coast.

When it eventually made landfall, the storm felled trees, swept away docks and piers, and twisted power lines in predictable fashion. But it was the incredible deluge of rain that fell along the hurricane's path that would place this storm in the record books.

According to the National Weather Service, its rainfall "produced the heaviest runoff of record on downstream tributaries and coastal creeks in North Carolina. The combination of tide waters from the east and floodwater from the west inundated the greatest area of eastern North Carolina ever known to have flooded."

But this was not 1999, and the storm was not Hurricane Floyd. Nor was it Fran in 1996, or Hazel in 1954. The year was 1955, and the hurricane was Ione.

Since the days of the first European explorations along the Carolina coast, sailors and settlers have recorded the effects of countless tropical storms and hurricanes. Unknown and unnamed storms have overwashed our coast and battered our state through the centuries, and many North

Carolinians have lost their lives in the desperate struggle against water and wind. Our collective hurricane memory, however, only spans a few generations, as stories of great storms of the past are handed down by our parents and grandparents. Many still talk about Hazel and the other storms of the fifties, and we will surely retell our ordeals with recent hurricanes. But there are countless disastrous storms in our state's stormy past that are now long forgotten.

While we may like to think that our recent hurricane misfortunes are a freak of nature or an anomalous cross of weather and geography, the fact is that North Carolina has always been a prime target for tropical weather. In the U.S., only Florida and Texas have seen more hurricane landfalls in the last one hundred years. And quite often, our storms have come in flurries—multiple hurricanes striking over a span of just a few years, followed quite mysteriously by decade-long periods of very little activity.

This pattern was certainly in place during the 1950s, when North Carolina was hammered by a series of storms that dispelled all statistical expectations. During this period seven hurricanes struck within roughly two years, including the most powerful of the state's twentieth century storms— Hurricane Hazel. Also among this cluster were Hurricanes Connie, Diane, and Ione, the trio of storms that landed within one frightening six-week period in 1955. More hurricanes came in the following years, including Hurricane Donna in 1960, which also made a direct hit as a major storm. After enduring what seemed like an unending string of cyclones, it's easy to see why the press dubbed eastern North Carolina "Hurricane Alley."

And then things changed dramatically. Throughout the next three decades, only a handful of hurricanes even threatened the Tar Heel coast, and even fewer actually made landfall. For almost twenty-five years, coastal residents went about their lives with barely a mention of hurricane watches or evacuation plans. This extended period of quiet was surely a blessing, but it also happened to coincide with an era of unprecedented development along the coast.

It was during the late fifties and early sixties that our beaches and resort communities began to grow rapidly. Coastal towns prospered, new roads were built, barrier islands became readily accessible, and a burgeoning economy brought a modern staple of affluence—a cottage at the beach— within reach of a broader population. Each summer, newly-laid highways fed streams of cars to the coast, and a blossoming tourism economy bolstered growth all around. The trend continued throughout the 1970s, '80s, and '90s, when our barrier islands became packed with surf shops, seafood restaurants, time-share condos and, on some beaches, multi-million dollar homes.

But then the storms returned. In the late 1980s, a few serious storms caught our attention in dramatic fashion. Hurricane Gloria swept the Outer Banks in 1985, but it was the ominous approach of Hurricane Hugo in 1989 that delivered the true wake-up call. Hugo eventually missed the North Carolina coast, turned inland just above Charleston, South Carolina, and left record destruction in its wake ($7 billion in the U.S., a record at that time). From the battered South Carolina coast to the downtown streets of Charlotte, Hugo redefined our understanding of what a powerful hurricane can do when it tracks inland.

However, Hugo was just a warm-up for the barrage of powerful and destructive storms that would strike in the 1990s. Of course there was Hurricane Andrew in 1992, which shattered all records for destruction ($25 billion) when it rolled across South Florida and later struck Louisiana. Then through the mid-'90's all eyes were on North Carolina again, at a time when record numbers of hurricanes were bred in the tropics. We suffered through close calls with Bob in 1991 and Felix in 1995. Media attention once again focused on Atlantic hurricanes and the far-reaching consequences of an active *La Niña*. Then the 1996 season delivered Bertha and Fran to the Tar Heel coast, a one-two punch unlike any seen here in over forty years.

After Fran's destructive march across the state, it was quickly recognized as our new benchmark for hurricane destruction. With a damage toll of more that $5 billion, Fran was easily the costliest disaster in the state's history, and the first "real hurricane" for an entire generation of North Carolinians. And, it was the storm that many had said was long overdue.

But then came more hurricanes. Bonnie swept ashore in 1998; then Dennis, Floyd and Irene pummeled the state in 1999. Floyd was the true disaster of this group, creating the greatest flood event in state history and killing more North Carolinians (51) than any hurricane of the twentieth century. With dollar losses estimated at more than $6 billion, Floyd has clearly surpassed Fran as our state's worst hurricane disaster.

Six hurricanes striking the same small portion of coastline within less than four years should be enough to impress any weather historian. But the real story here is not just the clustering of several storms in one state at the end of the century. Instead, this era will be remembered by the epic losses of life and property found in the wakes of Floyd and Fran. Like Hazel and Hugo before them, these powerful and awesomely destructive hurricanes were unkind to the coast. But with both storms, huge dollar damages and most of the storm-related deaths occurred inland, far away from the barrier beaches and battered condos. It's clear that we can no longer afford to think of hurricanes as merely coastal events.

So what should we expect with the next great storm?

Whether we want to acknowledge it or not, we know that sooner or later North Carolina will be hit by another major hurricane. It could be this year, or it could be thirty years from now. No forecast can tell us when the next "big one" will come. Some researchers are suggesting, however, that we have entered a multi-decade cycle of increased tropical activity in the Atlantic that could last for another twenty years. Does this mean that North Carolina should expect more Frans and Floyds right around the corner? Not necessarily. But we have clearly entered an era of multi-billion dollar storms, and we should recognize that when another major hurricane does hit, the losses will be great—especially if it tracks inland.

Forecasters, emergency managers, and government officials are working to mitigate for that next disaster, thereby reducing its potential impact. In some areas flood-prone properties have been bought out, and in others areas older, weaker structures have been replaced with newer, better-built ones. These and other similar efforts can have a significant effect on future storm dollar losses. And we can all do our share. We can benefit by making solid hurricane plans, by knowing the effects of flooding in our communities, by educating ourselves about evacuations, and by gaining a greater understanding of North Carolina's hurricane history.

Jay Barnes

Jay Barnes is author of *North Carolina's Hurricane History* (1995, 1998) and *Florida's Hurricane History* (1998), both published by the University of North Carolina Press (Chapel Hill, 800-848-6224). A native of Southport, he resides in Carteret County where he is director of the North Carolina Aquarium at Pine Knoll Shores. For more information on Barnes' hurricane books, visit his hurricane history website: http://metalab.unc.edu/uncpress/hurricanes/.

Storms Surge

By

Ben Steelman

First Bertha and Fran in 1996. Then Bonnie last year. Then Dennis and Floyd, with a threat of more hurricanes on the horizon.

"It's as if God set up a giant target out in the Atlantic Ocean off Wilmington and told his storms to try to hit it," joked Dr. John A. Clizbe, the American Red Cross's national vice president for emergency services.

State Sen. Patrick Ballantine noted that his daughter, at barely one month old, was already a veteran of two hurricanes.

Joshing aside, Lower Cape Fear residents have to look at the 1960s, '70s, and '80s with no nostalgia.

Between Hurricane Donna in 1960 and the awful autumn of 1996, the only storms to visit the southeastern North Carolina coast were Ginger, a weak category one hurricane that came ashore near Atlantic Beach, and Diana, which hit the Brunswick beaches in 1984. (Hugo, an intense category four storm, threatened to land near Cape Fear but veered to strike Charleston, S.C. in 1989.)

So what changed? What's going on here?

Some people have suggested that global warming, by further heating the Atlantic Ocean, might be breeding more, and more violent, hurricanes. The Environmental Defense Fund's web site raises the specter of storm surges flooding even the Capitol building in Washington.

Scientists who study hurricanes closely, however, are skeptical of that theory.

"The past has shown that this is a multi-decade cycle," said Tom Matheson, a meteorologist with the National Weather Service at Wilmington. "Global warming is apparently not the cause," he added.

"Some call it the 'North Atlantic oscillation,' some call it the 'conveyor-belt mechanism,'" said Dr. Sathu Raman, a professor at N.C. State University who is also North Carolina's state climatologist. "In any event, it is a 10-to-15-year cycle."

"To the best of anyone's knowledge, there simply is no direct relationship" between global warming and hurricanes, said historian Jay Barnes, director of the N.C. Aquarium at Pine Knoll Shores and author of *North Carolina's Hurricane History*.

"There have been other periods when many hurricanes have struck the coast," Mr. Barnes said. The most notorious was the period from 1953 to 1960, when nine hurricanes–including the fearsome Hazel–either landed or came dangerously close to the Cape Fear coast. That was the period when North Carolina was known as "Hurricane Alley."

Unfortunately, there is nothing unusual about two hurricanes buffeting the state in the same year, Mr. Barnes said. In fact, nine seasons in this century have seen two hurricanes. In 1955, three hit: Connie, Diane and Ione.

(The 1996 season nearly saw three hurricanes as well, Mr. Matheson noted. In addition to Bertha and Fran, a tropical storm named Arthur also affected the Carolina coast.)

What causes the hurricane cycle? Meteorologists, scientists who study the weather, tell a complex story.

Part of that story involves two Hispanic imps, "El Niño" and "La Niña." Another part involves the Bermuda High–which has nothing to do with Jimmy Buffet or naughty behavior.

El Niño, Spanish for "the little boy," is the folk nickname for a periodic disruption of winds and waters in the tropical Pacific Ocean. During this period, ocean waters become warmer and more turbulent; coastal floods may strike Peru, droughts can parch Indonesia and Australia and fishing catches decline.

For the American coast, however, the most notable effect is a collection of strong winds, also known as "the tropical jet," which cut across the Pacific into the Atlantic, and into the breeding grounds of some of the worst hurricanes, the waters off the Cape Verde Islands near Africa.

"A hurricane is like a big baby," Mr. Matheson said. "It requires an incubator." The storms breed in conditions of heat, of placid east-to-west winds and an absence of wind shear. "Everything's got to be just right."

The tropical jet, however, "rips those storms apart," he added. Relatively few hurricanes can form, and those that do are relatively weak. In 1997, when the last El Niño was at its height, North Carolina saw no hurricanes at all, Dr. Raman said.

However, El Niño does not last forever. After a few years, it is succeeded by La Niña, Spanish for "the little girl." In La Niña conditions, waters in the tropical Pacific are colder than usual-and no tropical jet disrupts storm formation off the Cape Verde islands.

Climate experts say the Pacific entered a La Niña phase in late 1998, and that conditions have persisted.

Related to this El Niño/La Niña cycle is a periodic warming and cooling of the Atlantic Ocean.

In the late 1940s through the early 1960s, for example, Atlantic waters were growing progressively warmer, Mr. Matheson said.

This was the period that coincided with the epoch of storms like Hazel, Connie and Donna.

In contrast, from about 1970 until the mid-1990s, the Atlantic enjoyed a relatively cool period, with "little intense storm activity," Mr. Matheson said.

The hurricanes that did emerge, such as Ginger or Donna, were relatively weak storms; Hugo was an anomaly.

In fact, the years 1991 to 1994 showed the least hurricane activity on record, he added.

However, "things really took off in 1995," Mr. Matheson said. Atlantic waters began warming again-and the storms began rolling.

A hurricane can be understood as a massive heat exchange.

The sun's heat evaporates water from the Atlantic, which forms gigantic clouds of moisture. The energy of that moisture's evaporation and condensation lowers atmospheric pressure, building stronger and stronger wind—"turning and turning in a widening gyre," in the words of the poet William Butler Yeats.

At Colorado State University, meteorologist William M. Gray has developed a fairly successful scheme for predicting hurricanes, based on the impact of such factors as above-average rainfall in Africa, the level of high-altitude winds and wind-shear in the tropical Atlantic, ocean temperatures in the Atlantic and the impact of El Niño/La Niña.

The 1999 forecast by Dr. Gray and his colleagues predicts 14 tropical storms strong enough to be named, nine hurricanes and four intense hurricanes in the Atlantic.

Unfortunately, Dr. Gray's forecasts can't tell where those storms will go. That depends on another set of variables-most notably, the Bermuda High, a persistent mass of high atmospheric pressure in the mid-Atlantic Ocean.

When temperatures in the Atlantic are relatively low, the Bermuda High shifts southward, and it tends to deflect any tropical storms toward the Gulf of Mexico, Mr. Matheson said. When temperatures are high, however, the Bermuda High heads north, and the way is clear for hurricanes to glide toward Florida or points northward on the Atlantic Seaboard.

"It's just been brutally bad luck for all these storms to head for North Carolina," Mr. Matheson said. Unfortunately for coastal residents, headed, these storm-friendly conditions are likely to persist well into the first decade of the 21st century. "We may be in for more of the same for several years," Dr. Raman said.

The condensation of one gram of rainwater expands about 580 calories of hear. When multiplied by about 20 billion tons of water–the amount of rainfall in a moderately strong hurricane in a 24-hour period–the result can be the release of energy equivalent to two Hiroshima bombs within a matter of seconds, Mr. Matheson said.

Complicating matters in Floyd's case was a low pressure system that drifted from the west and helped push the hurricane back out to sea, said meteorologist Ryan Boyles of the State Climate Office in Raleigh.

Floyd's combination of torrential rains with relatively modest winds reminded Dr. Raman of the tropical monsoons he studied in his native India. Such storms frequently cause disastrous flooding and loss of life in India, Pakistan and Bangladesh.

Many scientists believe that added CO_2 in the atmosphere is creating a "greenhouse effect," trapping solar heat and raising average temperatures worldwide.

Proponents of this theory–which include President Clinton and Vice President Al Gore–point to evidence that world temperatures have risen by about one degree Centigrade (about 1.8 degree Fahrenheit) in the past 20 years.

This warming, they caution, could melt more of the polar icecaps and the glaciers scattered around the globe, raising sea levels and placing more of the coastline at risk from the storm surges caused by hurricanes.

"Unless we change course, most scientists believe the seas will rise so high they will swallow whole islands and coastal areas," President Clinton said in a Sept. 15 speech in New Zealand.

Janine Bloomfield, senior scientist with the Environmental Defense Fund, does not paint so clear a picture as the president. Hurricanes are affected by climatic cycles, she admitted. However, warmer waters at the ocean's surface could produce stronger storms, though not necessarily more of them.

"It's a long-term trend," Dr. Bloomfield said. Hurricane Floyd cannot be blamed on the greenhouse effect, she said, "but it's similar to what computer models say could happen more often in the future."

However, critics question some of the evidence of global warming. Recent satellite data from NASA found no systematic warming in the troposphere, the lowest 10 miles of the Earth's atmosphere. In the stratosphere, the next highest level, average temperatures have actually declined in recent years; December 1997 was the coldest month ever recorded in the stratosphere, NASA reported.

Moreover, global warming, if it existed, might actually serve as a damper on hurricanes, Mr. Matheson speculated. Cold, fresh water from icebergs and glaciers could lower the temperature of ocean waters, making it harder for hurricanes to form, he said.

On the other hand, Nicholas Bates of the Bermuda Biological Station for Research suggests that hurricanes could stir up some of the carbon dioxide that is now dissolved in the ocean, pumping the gas back into the atmosphere and possibly contributing to the greenhouse effect.

Chris Landsea of the National Oceanic and Atmospheric Administration's hurricane research division told *The Christian Science Monitor*, such speculation was "overplayed."

Any warming-induced change in the number or strength of hurricanes would likely be "lost in the noise" of the year-to-year changes of the normal hurricane cycles, he said.

All efforts to "tame" hurricanes by artificial means have failed, Dr. Raman said. "That means all we can really do is build better buildings and heed the warnings."

By Ben Steelman, *Wilmington Morning Star*, September 26, 1999, (c) 1999 *Wilmington Morning Star*. Used by permission.

Ben Steelman

Ben Steelman went through Hurricane Hazel as a 5-month-old in Louisburg, N.C. A graduate of the University of North Carolina at Chapel Hill, he has worked for the *Wilmington Star-News* since 1977. His articles have appeared in *The Philadelphia Inquirer*, the *North Carolina Literary Review, Southern Cultures, North Carolina Historical Review* and elsewhere.

Hurricane Alley: When Will We Ever Learn?

By

Jim Stephenson

Hurricanes are no strangers to North Carolina. From 1990 to 1999, the National Hurricane Center reported eleven direct hits of major hurricanes to North Carolina, the same number as the eastern coast of Florida. Eight out of these eleven hurricanes hit North Carolina during the month of September. As Hurricane Floyd buffeted the Bahamas on September 13, many North Carolinians were quietly wishing that the storm would head due west. But it didn't. After brushing by Florida, Georgia and South Carolina, Floyd came ashore near Cape Fear during the early morning hours of September 16.

Eastern North Carolina was still soaked from a week long encounter (Aug. 30 to Sep. 5) with Hurricane Dennis that lingered off Cape Hatteras for days before making a return visit to the mainland at Cedar Island. By the time Hurricane Floyd rushed through the state, the rivers were already swollen and the soils saturated. There was nowhere for Floyd's waters to go.

Hurricane Floyd has been tagged the worst disaster in North Carolina history. Governor Hunt has estimated the damage at $5 billion. Whole towns were inundated by flood waters carrying everything from gasoline and oil slicks to hog carcasses and caskets downstream. Water collected in the floodplains of the Tar, Neuse, Cape Fear and Roanoke Rivers and displaced, and in some places destroyed, the communities and industries that built in these fragile areas.

Along the coast, the barrier islands protected the mainland from Hurricane Floyd's wrath.

Oak Island had the greatest structural damage from Floyd, with forty homes and vacation properties severely damaged or destroyed. Erosion on Bogue Banks, including Emerald Isle, Pine Knoll Shores and Atlantic Beach, caused the beach to migrate from fifteen to fifty feet landward. On Emerald Isle, one hundred and sixty homes are imminently threatened. Portions of Topsail, Oak, Surf City and North Topsail islands experienced ocean overwash and oceanfront dunes and berms built in the aftermath of Hurricane Fran were washed away.

Troubled Waters

Hurricanes Dennis and Floyd caused pollutants to flush into rivers, streams and sounds from flooded wastewater treatment plants, inundated septic systems, engulfed hog lagoons, underwater junkyards, drifting propane and oil tanks, and chemicals leaching from flooded garages and industrial facilities. This toxic soup has been transported downstream where it will deposit into estuaries of the Albemarle and Pamlico Sounds.

A plume of chocolate-colored sediment could be seen pushing its way into the Pamlico Sound from the Pamlico and Neuse Rivers. These pollutants may cause massive algal blooms that could last well into next year. Hans Paerl, a marine scientist at the University of North Carolina's marine lab, said, "We found low oxygen 'dead zone' conditions in bottom waters in a region of the sound under the influence of sediment plume."

Water quality deteriorated so badly during the storms that State Health Director Dennis McBride issued an advisory for people to avoid contact with the water that would expose eyes, ears, nose, mouth and any cuts or sores to floodwaters. Out on barrier islands, rain flooded low-lying neighborhoods. Island towns pumped the stormwater into the ocean, contributing to water quality degradation that in one case caused six surfers to become ill while swimming off Emerald Isle.

Raging Bulldozers

No sooner had Floyd passed than Outer Banks towns revved up the bulldozers. In the Town of Sunset Beach, the National Guard bulldozed the beach at the request of the town within days of the storm's passage. A guardsman serving on the town's police force led the effort to build a levy in violation of state and federal laws, even thought the beach had little damage. At Wrightsville Beach, the town began sculpting the beach before gaining the necessary approvals, as did Bald Head Island. All three towns have received notices of violation. At Caswell Beach, the National Guard did not succumb to pressure and valiantly held off attempts by the town to bulldoze until all of the permits were in order.

Since bulldozing can exacerbate beach erosion, federal and state approvals are necessary. Governments and property owners in beach communities are not allowed to begin bulldozing to repair dunes without first consulting the state Division of Coastal Management (DCM) and the U.S. Fish and Wildlife Service. "In each of the reported cases, the bulldozing was gratuitous, because there wasn't a real emergency," said Donna Moffitt, director of DCM. "Structures were not imminently threatened," she said.

In response to Hurricanes Dennis and Floyd, DCM created an emergency general permit for rebuilding property damaged or destroyed by the storms in coastal estuarine areas. The general permit does not apply to oceanfront structures. The temporary measure will expedite permit issuance, defer permit fees for hurricane repair work and waive the requirement that property owners notify adjacent property owners before rebuilding. A permit is needed when the damage to a structure is greater than fifty percent of the structure's value.

Dollars & Sense

When Hurricane Fran hit the North Carolina coast in September 1996, political officials claimed that they had learned some lessons. FEMA Director James Lee Witt told *The News & Observer* that "If we're going to keep people out of harm's way and if we're going to cut costs from disasters, we're going to have to change the way we do business." The recovery from Hurricane Fran racked up a bill of $6 billion, including $211 million in FEMA public assistance grants and loans.

Among the FEMA expenditures after Fran was $4.6 million to erect a four-foot high bank of sand extending fifteen miles along the beach at Topsail Island. The sand dunes were virtually wiped out during Floyd, leaving wooden walkways arching over the now-flattened beach. Federal monies also went toward rebuilding beach houses, fishing piers and a high-rise hotel, further promoting development in vulnerable areas.

"Bad management decisions in 1996 will haunt us for generations to come," predicted Kevin Moody, a resource biologist with the U.S. Fish and Wildlife Service, which has responsibility for protecting the nests of endangered sea turtles. He spent several days surveying the damage on barrier islands following Hurricane Floyd. Moody surmised, "I didn't see any damage that was purely because of Floyd. It was all because we decided not to take the appropriate action in 1996."

Since the beginning of the Federal Flood Insurance Program in 1968 through 1997, FEMA estimates that one-third of the $8 billion in flood insurance payments went to property owners experiencing repeated losses. Now that entire towns have been devastated, the question is: How and where will these communities rebuild? The town of Princeville on the Tar River, which received the brunt of Floyd's flooding, has been inundated five times in the last hundred years.

Looking to avoid repeating past mistakes, environmental organizations developed a set of principles for disaster relief, which were sent to the NC Congressional Delegation, Governor Hunt and state legislative leaders. The principles call for removing wastewater treatment plants, intensive livestock operations and junkyards from floodplains. Public funds should be used to relocate homes and businesses away from flood-prone areas. Instead of paying for the reconstruction of homes in high-risk portions of barrier islands, public funds should be used to acquire areas unsuitable for development.

During an aerial tour of storm damage caused by Floyd, FEMA Director Witt claimed that in addition to the cost of human misery, "every dollar we've invested in relocation, we've saved two dollars." Accompanying Witt on the tour, Carolyn Browner, administrator of the U.S. Environmental Protection Agency put it more succinctly: "We should stay out of floodplains."

Multiple Hurricanes in North Carolina			
1893	**1899**	**1933**	**1944**
August 27-29	August 16-18	August 22-23	August 1
October 13	October 30-31	September 15-16	September 14

1954	1955	1996	1999
Carol (August 30)	Connie (August 12)	Bertha (July 12)	Dennis (Aug. 30-Sept. 5)
Edna (September 10)	Diane (August 17)	Fran (September 5-6)	Floyd (September 15-16)
Hazel (October 15)	Ione (September 19)		Irene (October 16-17)

In the Wake of Floyd . . .

- 51 people dead
- 48,000 people fled to 235 emergency shelters
- 217 caskets disinterred by flood waters
- 1.2 million people lost electricity

- 30,500 hogs, 2.1 million chickens, 737,000 turkeys, and 880 cattle perished
- $800 million loss in agricultural sector
- $89.4 million in losses to forestry

- 50,000 homes damaged in 39 counties
- Only 20% with Federal flood insurance

- 24 municipal sewage plants flooded
- 400,000 wells at risk
- 33 dams failed, 84 overflowed, 59 damaged
- 650 roads closed during flood
- 15 bridges destroyed
- 3900 underground storage tanks impacted
- 197 superfund sites (federally funded cleanup sites) in flooded area
- 355 hazardous waste sites in flooded area

N.C. Sierra Club • Southern Environmental Law Center • N.C. Environmental Defense Fund
N.C. Coastal Federation • Neuse River Foundation • Pamlico-Tar River Foundation
N.C. Audubon • N.C. Wildlife Federation • Conservation Council / N.C.

Principles to Guide Disaster Relief
to Reduce Future Damage and Protect the Environment

The winds and rains of Hurricane Floyd have devastated parts of eastern North Carolina, and now we must commit ourselves to rebuilding the communities, lives and livelihoods of North Carolinians. As we rightly rush to relieve the suffering and rebuild our communities, we must be guided by principles that will decrease public health threats, environmental destruction and property loss that we face in future natural disasters.

Those mistakes include building homes, businesses, farms, factories and sewage treatment plants where they—and the communities around them—are particularly vulnerable to nature's hazard. We have intensely developed our lands in sensitive ecological areas and destroyed our wetlands such that they are less capable of absorbing floodwaters. We cannot stop hurricanes, but we can rebuild wisely—in ways that help minimize the personal devastation and public costs from future storms.

Intensive efforts are now underway to secure state and federal emergency assistance. As the state moves forward to identify and secure these funds, the following principles must guide our decision making in these critical days and months ahead.

Principles to keep citizens out of harm's way

Remove sources of pollution from the 100-year floodplain.

1) Repair and relocate as necessary waste treatment facilities.

Public expenditures should focus on immediate repair of damaged municipal waste treatment facilities to resume service. All damaged facilities should be examined to assess the risk of future flooding. If a significant risk exists, all future public expenditures should be used to relocate and construct treatment facilities at appropriate sites, with back-up power for emergency situations.

Private industrial waste treatment facilities damaged by flooding should be assessed for future risk. If the risk is significant, they should be relocated to appropriate sites. The owners of these facilities should pay for necessary repair and relocation.

2) Do not rebuild or replace anaerobic lagoons for concentrated animal production facilities, but provide flexibility and incentives to use some public assistance for innovative technologies.
The state has committed to phasing out lagoons for the treatment and disposal of hog waste. It makes no sense to use public money to rebuild systems targeted for closure. Public expenditures for damaged concentrated animal production facilities should require treatment technologies that do not employ anaerobic lagoons.

3) Do not build or replace hog factories and other concentrated animal operations in the 100-year floodplain, in wetlands, or in prior converted wetlands.
Public financial assistance should not be provided for the repair or reconstruction of any component of a concentrated animal production facility located within the 100-year floodplain or wetlands. The state could consider the feasibility of purchasing such facilities for wetland or floodplain restoration

4) Relocate major pollution sources from the floodplain.
Some uses should be banned outright in the floodplain, such as junkyards and certain types of facilities storing hazardous waste or materials.

Reduce subsidies of risk.

1) Relocate homes and businesses in extreme flood-prone areas.
Public expenditures for flood damage for homes and businesses located within the 100-year floodplain should include financial assistance adequate to cover relocation rather than rebuilding in these flood-prone sites.

2) Restrict development in high-risk portions of barrier islands and beaches. Public expenditures for infrastructure repair or reconstruction should not induce or sustain development in high risk portions of barrier islands and beaches. To protect and maintain the public beach, federal and state financial assistance for repair of damaged homes should require strict compliance with oceanfront setbacks, with no reconstruction of structures damaged more than 50% of the value of the structure and in violation of the applicable setback. Public disaster assistance should be used to acquire barrier island areas that are unsuitable for development and subject to repeated extensive damage from storms and hurricanes.

Enhance our natural defenses against disaster.

1) Expand floodplain and wetland restoration programs.
Federal and state assistance offers a real opportunity to restore floodplains or wetlands in floodprone watersheds. Drainage and loss of wetlands and channelization of streams have increased the duration and severity of flooding. These expenditures should work in concert with relocation efforts.

2) Restore buffers to reduce flooding and protect water quality.

Improve future planning.

1) Reassess floodplain delineation to determine the accuracy of current planning assumptions.

2) Require local preparation of floodplain management plans.

3) Assess status of residential drinking water wells and coordinate funding to relocate substandard wells.

4) Coordinate the multiple sources of state and federal relief and infrastructure funding (such as FEMA, flood insurance, Clean Water Bonds, and FSA Emergency Loans) to assure that wise planning principles are consistently observed.

Jim Stephenson

Jim Stephenson joined the North Carolina Coastal Federation staff in July 1999 as Program Analyst. Jim is leading the Nucor litigation effort for NCCF, conducting research and investigative reporting of other issues and projects. With more than 21 years of public policy, environmental issue and nonprofit experience, Jim is one of the state's most experienced and respected environmentalists. From 1997 to June 1999, Jim served as Executive Director of the Pamlico-Tar River Foundation where he managed staff and operations and researched and analyzed policy and issue positions. He also served as Advisor to the Governor of Pennsylvania for eight years, providing research, information and guidance on policy issues. Jim holds a Bachelor of Arts degree from Gettsyburg College, P.A., and lives in the downeast coastal community of Gloucester.

Part II Environmental Impact

Strength in Reserve

By

Gregory Janicke

At first, it had seemed like a rough mound of sand and stubble of brush, something forgotten and dead. The Reserve lay listless across the creek. An occasional gull glanced at it.

I had come from Chicago. In 1967, I had walked for miles through 23 inches of blinding snow in a historic blizzard.

I had come from Kansas. Once, while driving home from Topeka, I saw a tornado poke its monstrous finger from deepening, pea-green skies.

In 1999, I moved to North Carolina. There, I saw the Rachel Carson Reserve in Beaufort for the first time. There, I met the hurricanes.

I had thought, at first, that Taylor's Creek was calm, that the Reserve slept at night and most of the day, that the coast was clear and the sea was still.

I was from the Midwest.

The Rachel Carson Reserve is made up of three estuarine islands and a large marsh complex. It is located between the mouths of the Newport and North rivers behind the Beaufort Inlet. Herb and shrub thicket communities grow on dredge material deposits; salt marsh cordgrass lines the borders. Barrier islands protect the low energy beaches, tidal flats and extensive marsh areas.

An interpretative volunteer showed me spartina, sea oats, firewheels and a toothache tree. Gray pellets of periwinkles clung to marsh grass like lookouts expecting a ship. The mud flats smelled of rotten eggs, which were hydrogen sulfide emissions from anaerobic bacteria. At one point, the Reserve shoreline seemed to come alive. Thousands of fiddler crabs scurried about, racing from our huge, intrusive footfalls.

The Reserve had passed the summer of '99 in long, dry days touched with an occasional staccato storm. With each new visit, I learned of a new element of life, in the air, on the land, under the water. There was no finer sight than an ibis drifting in white flight through a clear Carolina sky. Fiddler crabs danced in their sideways strut. On shore, I saw horseshoe crab casings and cannonball jellyfish that had somehow found their way from southern waters. I learned that North Carolina was at a crosscurrent of the Atlantic Ocean, the cold northern Labrador Current mixing with the warm Gulf Stream waters, producing an amazing intersection of flora and fauna. Palmettos lived side-by-side with live oaks.

I wasn't in Kansas anymore.

I found sand dollars, whelks, oysters and clams. It seemed that the Reserve was an intricate system of ebb and flow, day and night, life and death. The water was teeming with life, as was the sand itself, the mud, the brush, the trees, the very air. Each element depended on another. Some pieces of this living jigsaw puzzle were as delicate as a gull's feather, others as hard as a clamshell.

In September 1999, the hurricanes came.

The twins Dennis One and Dennis Two, as our family called them, struck with fury and persistence. Dennis lingered a week, then backtracked through Beaufort. Hurricane Floyd moved with its own mind along Florida, Georgia and South Carolina. The picture on the Weather Channel made it seem like a vast buzzsaw blade, gnawing the coastline with impossible force. It struck Beaufort in the dark hours. Our family sat and watched the Weather Channel and local TV news stations explain what was happening. At one point, it sounded as if a train had run amok above us, racing through a deep tunnel of its own making.

Finally, the electricity dipped and failed. We sat in the rushing darkness with candles, flashlights and portable radios. I heard the swoosh and thud of a tree falling near the house. Pinecones peppered the roof. After long hours, we walked outside to a fuzzy dawn. Tall trees had uprooted. Water choked gullies, ditches, any available nook and cranny. Along the streets, there was a mad interlace of fallen branches. A gas station sign was twisted into a metal Mobius strip. High winds had pitched a children's playground across the highway.

At a family house along the river, a pier had come undone. Sixty-foot pilings lay in the yard, one a few feet from the back deck. Tall pines had fallen on power lines. The yard itself was lost in an insane carpet of debris.

Along the Beaufort seafront, countless trees and branches lay scattered. A rowboat had been casually tossed across a street. Planks on piers had vanished. Muddy brown water swirled inches under the boardwalk.

After Floyd, there was slight respite, then more rain. In what seemed a blink of time, Hurricane Irene poured even more rain.

Finally, there was sun.

From the Beaufort boardwalk, the Reserve looked battered. It seemed as if there had been a fire amongst the trees and shrubs. Salt spray from the hurricanes had burned vegetation. Trees had uprooted from the wet soil, high tides and gusty winds. Trees that had seen decades of history had fallen and died, their fingering roots useless.

The shoreline had shifted, as if some great hand had scooped the sand and had flung it to the caprice of wind. The vast amount of water pushing through the inlet had lowered, raised and completely reshaped the shore. There were major fluctuations in water depth, salinity and turbidity. The west-end beach had experienced two feet of erosion. Bird Shoals was flattened by the relentless wash of water.

Surrounding water remained the color of oil and tea for more than a month.

The long-range effects of the hurricanes have yet to be determined. Scientists are investigating wind and water, large masses of matter and microscopic organisms. According to NASA, scientists are studying the effects of Floyd and subsequent rains on phytoplankton and algae blooms through use of NASA's Earth-orbiting Sea-viewing Wide Field-of-view Sensor (SeaWiFS) and an airborne laser instrument. Pat Tester, a NOAA scientist at the Center for Coastal Fisheries and Habitat Research in Beaufort, has coordinated sampling missions from small boats on regional waterways with flights by a NOAA Twin-Otter aircraft carrying the NASA laser and observations from the SeaWiFS spacecraft.

Larry B. Crowder, a professor of marine biology at the Duke University Marine Laboratory, reported in a Duke publication that he and other researchers expect the environmental impacts from hurricanes Dennis, Floyd and Irene to provide unique data. Crowder and assisting graduate students have discovered a new low-oxygen zone covering a 40-square-mile radius in Pamlico Sound. Similar zones have been found in the Neuse River. According to Crowder, these zones occur when fresh water is dumped into the sound from upstream estuaries and sits atop salt water, cutting it off from atmospheric mixing. Without sufficient oxygen, fish are forced into different parts of the water column. They must compete with other marine life for scarce food. Low oxygen zones cause some marine life to die, reducing the food source for many fish.

The power and fury of the hurricanes of '99 show that the Rachel Carson Reserve is a living system, rising and falling, shifting and regrouping after the assault of wind and water. It is a sponge absorbing excess runoff from land, a buffer protecting the mainland from storms. It is an interdependent web of life, torn up and cast about by the hurricanes, yet able to demonstrate amazing resiliency.

It is a vital filtering system at the point where rivers meet the sea.

Gregory Janicke

Gregory Janicke is a published environmental writer, playwright, artist and illustrator. He lives in Beaufort, North Carolina, where he operates Tall Trees Studio. He also serves as executive director of the Carolina Estuarine Reserve Foundation (www.ncnerr.org/cerf), a nonprofit organization supporting the North Carolina National Estuarine Research Reserve.

Shellfish

By

George Gilbert

Heavy rainfall events have always been a problem for both shellfishermen and the Shellfish Sanitation Program. The storm water runoff from heavy rains brings bacteria and other contaminants into coastal North Carolina's estuaries, and causes the temporary closure of various shellfish harvesting areas. Consequently, shellfish harvesters have either limited areas or no areas at all in which to work.

Heavy rains also bring about an increase in the Shellfish Sanitation staff's workload, since they must prepare all areas to reopen as soon as it is safe to do so. Staff members must collect a greater number of samples over a larger area of coverage. Since storm events require such active responses for sampling activities, routine requirements often fall behind schedule, and staff members must often work beyond the normal expectancy to meet program responsibilities. For instance, in coastal areas that are hit with flooding, our three laboratories gear up to help out county health departments test wells for bacterial contamination. Close to 650 drinking water samples were analyzed after Hurricane Floyd.

The types of concerns that hurricanes invoke for both shellfishermen and the Shellfish Sanitation Program are exemplified by the most recent series of hurricanes to strike the North Carolina coast. Due to Hurricane Dennis, the Shellfish Sanitation staff closed waters statewide on August 31, 1999. These waters reopened on September 10, only to be closed again five days later due to the effects of Hurricane Floyd. Partial reopenings occurred on October 6, by which point all shellfishing waters in the state had been closed for 21 days to obtain results from chemical and pesticide water sampling. Initial bacteriological sampling results indicated the effects on shellfishing waters to be minimal and short-lived.

On October 18, Hurricane Irene bombarded the coast with heavy rains. The resultant run-off caused additional closures of shellfishing waters. The final reopening, placing all areas back to normal boundaries, did not take place until October 30. Shellfish harvesting was therefore limited for a total of two months. Although these closures were temporary, they still should be considered as an aftermath of the storms causing lost wages for many shellfishermen statewide.

Currently, shellfish harvesting waters have been restored to their normal conditions. Still, though their effects were temporary, these three hurricanes took their toll.

George Gilbert

George Gilbert is Section Chief of the Shellfish Sanitation and Recreational Water Quality programs of the Division of Environmental Health of the Department of Environment and Natural Resources.

Creek Dwellers in Crisis:
Flooding and the Inhabitants of the Northeast Cape Fear

By

Andy Wood

A few days after Floyd struck our area, I went out to a creek just north of Wilmington to see what it was doing. The creek flows into the Northeast Cape Fear river a little less than a mile from where I was exploring it. As expected, the creek was flowing hard and fast from all the drainages upstream. I was pleased to see however that the water flowing by was clear—though stained a dark tea color, the result of pigment leached from leaves and other plant matter. The pigment, called tannin, is harmless and is a common trait among our coastal plain ponds and rivers. When combined with water, tannins form a weak acid solution called tannic acid. This natural chemical process gives the water a slightly acid pH; again, a natural condition and one that is preferred by a great number of aquatic plants and animals.

During previous visits to this particular stretch of creek, I had seen numerous kinds of animals typically found in the Northeast Cape Fear. Largemouth bass, bluegill sunfish and the guppy-like mosquitofish are all quite common there.

Because the water was flowing clear, not clouded by silt or sediment, I could tell the drainage area feeding the torrent was well-protected from erosion. In fact, I knew some of the habitat that the water had come from: mostly bottom-land swamp, longleaf pine forest and some open grassy areas. This is where the tannins came from—a relatively undeveloped area, since the land is low and used mainly for forestry. Some of the most interesting features in the upstream drainage are several small pocket ponds that dot the landscape and are not connected to any stream or to each other during times of normal water levels. These isolated ponds are unique characters, as no two are alike. Some have fish, which indicates they have water year-round; others lack fish but support a wealth of amphibians, including treefrogs, toads and salamanders.

While I have a keen interest in fishless ponds because of my love of amphibians, some of the pocket ponds that do have fish are equally interesting because of the kinds of fish they harbor. Instead of common bluegill and bass, these small ponds harbor such oddities as mudminnows, banded sunfish, pygmy sunfish and redfin pickerel. These are all small species in keeping with the small ponds they live in. The pygmy sunfish grows to just over an inch long, and a huge redfin pickerel will be a foot long—a dwarf compared to its similar-looking cousins, the pike and muskellunge. Because the ponds are isolated from other waters, the animal communities in them, be they fish or amphibians, have developed their unique makeup over a long period of time.

Standing on the shore of the now-raging creek, I could not avoid the opportunity to dipnet the shoreline to see what animals I could find. Along with the expected handful of ubiquitous mosquitofish, I was surprised to catch up a pocket pond-dwelling mudminnow. But the next swipe I took, in a tangle of sweetgum tree branches, yielded a truly unexpected catch: broken striped newts. Two of them. I have collected newts in big and small ponds before but this aquatic salamander rarely if ever spends time in rivers. It is most often found in pocket ponds like those found in the drainage area at the creek where I stood. Successive netting revealed no less than seven of the amphibians, all in that one area of submerged tree branches. They clustered there because it was the first safe haven they could find after being spilled out into the open creek from a large drainage culvert a short distance away.

The proof of my hypothesis was evidenced not so much by the mudminnow, which can be found in swamps along our rivers, but rather by the newts, which do not normally inhabit our rivers' swamps. The newts are indicator species of pond habitats. Their presence in a flooded creek means their former home must also be flooded. And here is where the study of our unique wetlands and aquatic habitats really gets interesting. Just when we get to a point where the ecological makeup of a particular pond seems understood, along comes a flood to mix everything up. Where once a pond had no fish, it now has many. The newts and other amphibians swept into an undesirable stream habitat now must cross overland in hopes of finding a new suitable pond habitat. So, a process last begun centuries ago—or whenever a flood of this magnitude last occurred—is being repeated. It is a tragedy for some animal communities, but an opportunity for others. And the truly wondrous thing about it for me is, I am here to watch the drama unfold.

Will the Solutions We're Looking for Prove Detrimental to the Health of Our Waterways?

Flooding plagues us here in southeastern North Carolina. It is a problem we have helped create by paving square miles of land that would otherwise absorb stormwater, and building constructs in places that historically functioned as wetlands. Nearly sixty percent of New Hanover County's soils are officially classified as hydric or wetland-type soil. Hydric soils are recognizable to the unaided eye because they consist largely of decomposed organic matter and hence are generally dark brown to black in color. The organic matter is basically the remains of ancient trees, mosses and other plant matter. Because of its makeup, this type of soil functions beautifully as a natural sponge, some soils soaking up to five times their weight in water.

The nature of other wetland soils may be a little less obvious because they contain sand or clay and seem to drain well near the surface. In many places around here, though, surface conditions may be deceiving; beneath good-looking soils there may lie a layer of impervious clay, a so-called aquatard that prevents water from percolating down through the soil profile. Where aquatards are present, we generally see pockets of standing water following rain events. The trained eye can often determine aquatard zones by the presence of certain wetland adapted plants, including cypress trees, certain mosses, ferns, and a variety of shrubs such as the zenobia bush, dahoon holly, and cyrilia.

Flooding in these places is not new, nor is it a problem—that is, until we put something in them that is not adaptable to flooding: for example, houses, stores and roads. Knowing that sixty percent of the county's soil is wetland by nature, and that roughly thirty-plus percent of the county is already covered with some kind of impervious surface—roads, parking lots, buildings, et cetera—it requires little thought to figure out where the existing constructs lie and why the new constructs seem to be prone to flooding. The old stuff is built on the highest, driest land, which means the new stuff must be fit onto marginally well-draining soils or wetland soils that have been drained and covered over by sand and topsoil.

This latter strategy strikes me as being akin to placing a dinner plate on a kitchen sponge; it may rest there, but it is none too stable, and where once there was a sponge there most certainly had to have been water as well. Paving over the sponge merely forces the inevitable stormwater to go elsewhere, all fifty-two-plus inches we can expect in a typical year. This is a big reason why so many established areas that never experienced flooding before are now seeing it on a regular basis. It's a critical mass phenomenon where the runoff from adjacent developments combines to form a volume of water much greater than that which would be expected from a single site.

But flooding is only one of the symptoms of our growth problems. Water quality is also compromised when wetlands are taken out of commission. This is because in addition to storing water, wetlands also cleanse stormwater. The natural carbon in the organic soil acts as a filter for contaminants such as petrochemicals. Bacteria in the soil also work on such chemicals, along with fertilizers and other nutrients. Even the living wetland plants aid in maintaining water quality. Their roots hold the soil in place, keeping silt and sediment from rushing into creeks and rivers. Silt and sediment clog fishes' gills, smother shellfish, and carry a variety of chemicals and bacteria that we don't want washing into our waters.

The value of wetlands is best appreciated when you understand that nearly seventy percent of the pollution entering our waters is of a non-point source: that is, pollution that comes off the land rather than from a point-source discharge pipe. The wetlands intercept and treat much of the contaminated stormwater before it reaches our groundwater and surface creeks—and they do it for free. The last estimate I heard for the county's stormwater correction efforts had a price tag in excess of 110 million dollars. And that for only a few developments.

We need to look at how we are managing our remaining wetlands, implement greater safeguards that will ensure their continued function, and then evaluate where we expect to be in fifty years, so that a plan for growth can be designed as a community with common needs and values.

Photo credit: Wilmington-Star News / Erin Wall

Andy Wood

Andy Wood studied Resource Conservation at Texas A&M University. He presently serves as Curator of Education for the North Carolina Aquarium at Fort Fisher. Andy's coastal wildlife commentaries can be heard each Wednesday on WHQR Public Radio. He and his wife operate a landscaping business called Habitats. They reside in Wilmington with their two sons, Robin and Carson.

Storms, Floodplain Development, and Water Pollution in the Cape Fear River

By

Michael A. Mallin

A Coastal Area in Nature's Crosshairs

Since 1996, the Cape Fear region of North Carolina has been battered by Hurricanes Bertha and Fran (1996), Bonnie (1998) and Dennis and Floyd (1999). Two of these storms (Bertha and Dennis) delivered glancing blows and passed northward up the coast. However, Hurricanes Fran, Bonnie, and Floyd led to considerable local economic loss and environmental damage.

I am a water quality scientist and direct the Aquatic Ecology Laboratory, a research group that is part of the University of North Carolina at Wilmington's Center for Marine Science Research. Since 1994, as part of the Lower Cape Fear River Program my laboratory has regularly sampled over 30 stations in the Cape Fear Estuary, the mainstem Cape Fear River, and the two major Coastal Plain tributaries, the Black and Northeast Cape Fear Rivers. We have accumulated an extensive amount of data regarding the environmental effects of these hurricanes, and we can now make some conclusions about the role humans play in making the inevitable storm damage even worse.

After Hurricane Bertha impacted Wilmington, it moved rapidly northward up the coast, passing over the New River and the City of New Bern. Water quality damage near Wilmington was limited to a narrow band along the coast. However, Hurricane Fran struck Wilmington with devastating force, and proceeded to follow the Cape Fear River upstream, where severe damage was incurred by the Piedmont cities of Raleigh and Greensboro, as well as many other municipalities.

The hurricane impacts in the upper watersheds of the mainstem Cape Fear River and its two principal tributaries, the Black and Northeast Cape Fear Rivers, led to major water quality problems downstream in the lower river reaches and the estuary.

We assess water quality by measuring a variety of indicators, including river dissolved oxygen, biochemical oxygen demand, nutrient (nitrogen and phosphorus) concentrations, and fecal coliform bacteria counts. A naturally occurring result of the heavy rains associated with hurricanes in the Southeast is the flooding of swamp water into river channels. Swamp water has naturally low levels of dissolved oxygen, and this flooding can cause river dissolved oxygen levels to drop. However, this natural drop in dissolved oxygen has been made much worse by certain human practices.

Hogs, Floodplain Development, and Other Human-Caused Pollution

A critical and repeated human consequence of hurricane events is loss of electric power to wastewater treatment plants and associated pump stations. If no independent backup generating source is available, these facilities are forced to reroute untreated or partially treated sewage into nearby waterways. During Hurricane Fran, approximately seventy million gallons of wastewater was thus diverted in the mainstem Cape Fear River basin, about four and a half million gallons in the Black River basin, and about 900,000 gallons in the Northeast Cape Fear River basin. Statewide, approximately 211 million gallons were diverted.

Wastewater contains nutrients, fecal bacteria, and an organic pollution load, called the biochemical oxygen demand (BOD). When a BOD load enters a water body, naturally-occurring bacteria feed on this organic material, utilizing the dissolved oxygen in the water for their normal respiration. When massive BOD loads enter water bodies, the dissolved oxygen concentration can drop to levels dangerous or fatal to the health of resident aquatic organisms, such as fish and shellfish. The rerouted human sewage load undoubtedly contributed to the very low dissolved oxygen levels persisting for days to months after Fran.

The Cape Fear watershed is the major swine-producing area in North Carolina. Numerous industrial-style hog farms (called concentrated animal operations, or CAOs) are located in the watershed, many on river floodplains. These systems utilize a waste disposal operation that pumps the feces and urine from thousands of confined hogs into an outdoor pond, called a lagoon. Swine waste, like human waste, contains high levels of nutrients, BOD, and fecal bacteria. The waste sits in the lagoon and undergoes some breakdown, and when the levels reach a certain height, the excess is pumped out and sprayed onto nearby fields. Plants in the field are supposed to take up the waste nitrogen, while the soils are supposed to absorb the phosphorus. However, research at North Carolina State University has shown that high levels of nutrients can enter nearby streams if it rains shortly after spraying.

Thus, another major source of BOD to the lower Cape Fear system after Fran was swine waste entering the streams and rivers from ruptured and inundated lagoons, as well as the spraying of waste onto fields already saturated by rainfall. There were four major lagoon accidents in the Northeast Cape Fear River basin and one in the Black River basin; statewide, there were 22 waste lagoon accidents after Fran.

The most severe and persistent drops in dissolved oxygen occurred in the Northeast Cape Fear River near the town of Castle Hayne. Here, data gathered by my laboratory personnel showed that there was virtually no dissolved oxygen from surface to bottom for nearly three weeks. There was also a massive fish kill at this location brought on by the lack of dissolved oxygen. Following Fran, dissolved oxygen levels returned to normal in about three weeks in the Cape Fear mainstem, in about six weeks in the Black River, but not for eight weeks in the Northeast Cape Fear River.

Why was the Northeast Cape Fear affected more strongly than the other two branches when it received by far the smallest human sewage load? Very likely because the Northeast Cape Fear received the heaviest swine waste load, with four major lagoon accidents. Data generated by agricultural engineers at North Carolina State University show that the BOD levels in swine waste liquid are approximately 750 mg/L (milligrams per liter, the same as parts per million) and in swine sludge it is much higher. Human sewage also contains dishwater, bathwater, and other "grey" water; consequently its BOD is much lower (about 200 mg/L). In fact, our sampling of the river near Castle Hayne showed BOD levels of 8.2 mg/L 12 days after Fran, while samples from the other main river branches were all less than 2.2 mg/L.

When Hurricane Bonnie impacted the Cape Fear region in 1998, our rivers again suffered considerable environmental damage. Again, swamps flooded into river channels. To assess the amount of pollution that swamp water alone can cause, our laboratory tested waters draining from a nearly pristine swamp (Colly Creek) and a watershed containing 95 concentrated animal operations (Great Coharrie Creek). We found that floodwater leaving Great Coharrie Creek contained twice the BOD, ten times the phosphorus, and 250X the fecal coliform bacterial concentrations as did water leaving Colly Creek. Thus, while swamp water does have low dissolved oxygen, it contains a much lower pollutant load than do waters draining a basin containing numerous large hog farms.

Our research has also indicated that pumping of liquid swine waste onto rain-saturated fields can produce a significant BOD impact on receiving stream water. Following Bonnie, our laboratory researchers noted that CAO operators in the upper Northeast Cape Fear River area were spraying large quantities of swine waste onto nearby fields from lagoons in danger of overtopping. Water samples collected just downstream of those areas produced BOD concentrations of 8-9 mg/L; farther downstream, where large amounts of human sewage entered the river, BOD ranged from 2-4 mg/L. In comparison, our three-year average BOD value in this river is 1 mg/L.

Risks to Human Health

Hurricanes are a danger to humans in more ways than the risks of physical injury or drowning. Human sewage and animal wastes contain microbes (bacteria, viruses, and protozoans) that can be pathogenic, or cause human illness. These microbial pathogens can enter the body through open wounds, or through the mouth, nose, and eyes. When large quantities of untreated sewage or animal wastes enter a stream or river, they can survive for a number of days in the turbid, nutrient-rich waters. They may also be transported far downstream from their source areas.

In the aftermath of Hurricane Bonnie, we extensively sampled streams and rivers for fecal coliform bacteria, organisms that are used by regulatory agencies such as the North Carolina Division of Water Quality as estimators of the degree of fecal microbial contamination. In North Carolina, streams and rivers are considered unsafe for human contact when fecal coliform bacteria counts exceed 200 colony-forming units (CFU) per 100 milliliters of water. Following Bonnie, several locations had counts ranging from ten to more than one hundred times this standard. These stations were located near wastewater treatment plants that had bypass incidents, in streams draining watersheds rich in CAOs, and throughout the Northeast Cape Fear River. If possible, it is important for citizens to avoid contact with river water for a period of at least three weeks after such events to avoid waterborne illnesses.

Another health problem can occur well after major storms. During large floods such as those occurring after Hurricane Floyd, many homes and businesses had standing water in them for days. Even in buildings that did not suffer severe structural damage, this water will encourage the growth of mold and other potentially noxious microbes. This presents a long-term danger to people with allergies or weakened immune systems who have to reoccupy these homes and businesses.

Dead Fish, Shellfish, and Other Marine Life

Dr. Martin Posey heads the Benthic Ecology Laboratory at UNC-Wilmington. Research by his group showed that in the wake of Hurricane Fran, the abundance of the organisms that live within the river sediments (collectively called the benthos) suffered sharp drops, not only in the Northeast Cape Fear River but in the estuary as well. Since many of these organisms serve as food for fish, maintaining a diverse and abundant benthic community is essential to the proper functioning of a river ecosystem. The benthos recovered to normal numbers in two to four months in most areas, with longest recovery times in a mid-estuary location and the Northeast Cape Fear River.

Dr. Posey's group has continued to follow the population dynamics of the Cape Fear benthic community since Hurricane Fran. They found that selected sampling stations also suffered severe benthos decreases after Hurricane Bonnie, including a station well downstream in the estuary, and once again, the Northeast Cape Fear River. In fact, the benthic community at that location had not recovered fully before Hurricane Floyd struck the area in 1999.

The major problem for benthic organisms is that they are forced to deal with extremely low dissolved oxygen levels brought on by the loading of BOD into the system. Since the movement of many of these organisms is very limited, if they cannot adapt to such situations they die. Another problem is flooding of freshwater. Even if the dissolved oxygen in a given location is sufficient, prolonged pulses of freshwater entering estuarine situations may kill or displace the normal brackish water benthic organisms.

Following Hurricane Fran, fish kills were large and widespread, but especially so in the lower Northeast Cape Fear River. Thousands of fish, including largemouth bass, sunfishes, flounders and hogchokers littered the surface and banks for days afterwards. A similar picture was evident after Hurricane Bonnie, where a conservative estimate of 10,000 dead fish was given for the Northeast Cape Fear River in the Castle Hayne region. The victims included largemouth bass, sunfishes, catfishes, hogchokers, blue crabs, crayfish, and even eels. During these incidents the drop in river dissolved oxygen was rapid, and the fish had no oxygenated refuge to escape to.

In contrast with these hurricanes, the aftermath of Hurricane Floyd led to only a small recorded fish kill that took place about three weeks after the event. Interestingly, all the carcasses we saw were adults; unlike previous kills, there were no juveniles present. We suspect that the smaller fish escaped into refuge zones in the flooded river floodplains, where they were able to escape the dangerously low dissolved oxygen while finding abundant food. A river ecology theory holds that periodic flooding is good for fish communities, because it gives the smaller fish access to rich food resources while simultaneously providing them with relative protection from larger river-ine predators among the floodplain vegetation.

What About the Future?

There will always be environmental damage associated with hurricanes. However, data from hurricanes in areas where there is relatively low human development (such as Cape Cod and the Florida Everglades), shows that such damage is less severe and long-lasting than in areas where there is extensive development (i.e. Miami, Charleston, and the Cape Fear and Neuse Rivers in North Carolina). One problem is the aforementioned power outages, which lead to rerouting or bypassing of poorly-treated human sewage into nearby water bodies. A solution to this problem is the installation of independent generating systems that will provide adequate power when the main lines go down. This can be an expensive undertaking, especially for smaller municipalities, but the risks to human health and the environment make it worthwhile.

Another major issue is development in floodplains. The most obvious issue is that of swine waste lagoons being located in these sensitive areas. The breaches and inundations of numerous lagoons following Fran and Floyd clearly demonstrated this problem. While recent legislation banned future lagoon construction from the 100-year floodplain, there remain hundreds of lagoons still located in these sensitive areas.

Hog waste spray fields are frequently located in floodplains as well. When heavy storms bring about excess rains that threaten to overtop waste lagoons, operators can legally pump and spray liquid waste onto rain-saturated fields. This allows for large amounts of waste to pass right over or through these saturated soils to nearby creeks, as our BOD, fecal coliform, and nutrient data have indicated. The recent legislation did not ban new spray fields from floodplains.

Floodplain development generally worsens the effect of hurricanes and floods. Many houses on river floodplains have septic tank systems that were flooded during the hurricanes, with consequent input of their wastes to the rivers. Floodplains contain wetlands that naturally absorb large quantities of water and filter pollutants. Whenever roads, businesses, houses, drives, and parking lots replace wetlands in these areas, this has the effect of diverting polluted floodwaters elsewhere instead of absorbing them into the soils. The massive flooding following Hurricane Floyd is an example of such an occurrence.

Atmospheric scientists say that we are in a hurricane "cycle" that could last ten to fifteen more years. From a water quality standpoint, it would be wise to take concerted action to remove pollution sources from floodplains, fit all sewage treatment plants with backup generators, save our remaining wetlands, and discourage further human development on floodplains. While some hurricane-caused environmental damage is inevitable, its extent and duration can be limited by taking such proactive measures.

Acknowledgments

Funding for the research discussed in this chapter was provided by the Lower Cape Fear River Program, the UNC-Wilmington Center for Marine Science Research, the Water Resources Research Institute of the University of North Carolina (Projects 70156 and 70171), and the Z. Smith Reynolds Foundation. I thank Jesse Cook, Scott Ensign, Jenny Johnson, Matt McIver, Doug Parsons, Chris Shank, Ashley Skeen and Tracey Wheeler for their invaluable field and laboratory efforts.

Suggestions for Further Reading

Burkholder, J.M., M.A. Mallin, H.B. Glasgow Jr., L.M. Larsen, M.R. McIver, G.C. Shank, N. Deamer-

Melia, D.S. Briley, J. Springer, B.W. Touchette and E. K. Hannon. 1997. Impacts to a coastal river and estuary from rupture of a swine waste holding lagoon. *Journal of Environmental Quality* 26:1451-1466.

Mallin, M.A. 2000. Impacts of industrial animal production on rivers and estuaries. *American Scientist* 88:26-37.

Mallin, M.A., M.H. Posey, G.C. Shank, M.R. McIver, S.H. Ensign and T.D. Alphin. 1999. Hurricane effects on water quality and benthos in the Cape Fear watershed: natural and anthropogenic impacts. *Ecological Applications* 9:350-362.

Tilmant, J.T., R.W. Curry, R. Jones, A. Szmant, J.C. Zieman, M. Flora, M.B. Robblee, D. Smith, R.W. Snow and H. Wanless. 1994. Hurricane Andrew's effect on marine resources. *BioScience* 44:230-237.

Valiela, I., P. Peckol, C. D'Avanzo, K. Lajtha, J. Kremer, W.R. Geyer, K. Foreman, D. Hersh, B. Seely, T. Isaji and R. Crawford. 1996. Hurricane Bob on Cape Cod. *American Scientist* 84:154-165.

Van Dolah, R.F. and G.S. Anderson. 1991. Effects of Hurricane Hugo on salinity and dissolved oxygen conditions in the Charleston Harbor. *Journal of Coastal Research* 8:83-94.

Michael A. Mallin

Michael Mallin was born in Cleveland, Ohio, where as a boy he saw firsthand the chemical pollution of the Cuyahoga River and massive algal blooms on Lake Erie. He received his Bachelor's degree in botany from Ohio University and worked for a time in wastewater treatment. He went on to earn a Master's degree in limnology from the University of Florida and studied reservoirs and rivers as a biologist in the power industry for several years. He then earned his Ph.D. in marine and estuarine ecology from the University of North Carolina at Chapel Hill.

He is currently Research Associate Professor at the University of North Carolina at Wilmington Center for Marine Science Research. He serves as Research Coordinator for the Lower Cape Fear River Program, the New Hanover County Tidal Creeks Project, and the Wilmington Watersheds Program. Dr. Mallin's recent research projects include studying the effect of land use practices on water quality, determining what nutrients limit nuisance algal growth in tidal creeks and urban lakes, assessing the effect of nutrient loading on the water quality of blackwater streams, studying the effect of catastrophic weather events on rivers and estuaries, analyzing environmental effects of concentrated animal operations on receiving waters, and determining environmental conditions favoring the growth of toxic dinoflagellate blooms.

Troubled Waters: Floyd's Flood Hurt Pamilico Sound Too

By

Larry Crowder and Todd Miller

Claiming that Pamlico Sound is fine now that a 40-square-mile low-oxygen zone has disappeared makes about as much sense as claiming that everything is fine in Kinston or Princeville now that houses and roads aren't flooded. The impacts of the hurricanes of 1999 on the North Carolina estuaries that produce nearly half the East Coast's fishes may be less visible than broken dikes and ruined homes, but the damage will likely be extensive and persistent.

Shortly after Hurricane Dennis skirted our coastline and churned off Cape Hatteras, Hurricane Floyd cut a swath across the coastal plain, dropping more than 15 inches of rain in saturated watersheds. Huge floods resulted, devastating much of eastern North Carolina. Modifications to the landscape-building roads and cities, ditching and draining farmland, and eliminating wetlands and streamside vegetation-may have contributed to the damage. Floyd flooded farms and cities, washed away houses and cars, and killed at least 50 people. It also inundated sewage treatment plants, hog waste lagoons and junkyards. The flooding grabbed national headlines and pictures conveyed the extent of human suffering. What they didn't reveal completely was how the flooding pushed the detritus of human civilization-our nutrients, human and livestock wastes, as well as toxic chemicals-downstream to Pamlico Sound.

Water quality problems plaguing the Neuse and Pamlico Rivers for decades have helped us understand the close connections between land use and water quality. Up to now, however, most believed that these problems did not extend to Pamlico Sound. While our polluted rivers still act as nurseries for seventy-five percent to eighty percent of recreational and commercial fishes, Pamlico Sound itself is doubly important as both habitat and major fishing grounds. Many young fish, including gag grouper, black sea bass and summer flounder, use the saltier waters of the sound, and nearly seventy-five percent of shrimp are landed there.

Right now the Neuse River is basically "freshwater-sunfish occupy habitat" that should be supporting sea trout and spot. The flood washed away any hope that the state's goal of a thirty percent nitrogen reduction can be achieved any time soon—nutrient reduction targets probably need to be increased if we want healthy fisheries.

Pamlico Sound now suffers from a spate of problems. Floating freshwater isolated salty bottom waters, reducing oxygen. The 40-square-mile low-oxygen zone persisted for three weeks, suffocating juvenile fish, shrimp and crabs. Then Hurricane Irene mixed oxygen back into Pamlico Sound and the media spread the good news.

But then the sick fish began showing up. Menhaden, spot, croaker, pinfish and others were found with open bleeding sores and deadly bacterial infections. Their skin and scales sloughed off and their stomachs swelled. Chances are slim they'll survive and grow in Floyd's nursery.

Nutrients have increased potentially problematic algae tenfold. The algae blooms would have been even larger, but Pamlico Sound is now stained like a blackwater river, blocking light that drives algal growth.

Cooling temperatures have temporarily calmed these troubled waters, but huge quantities of nutrients and organic wastes remain in Pamlico Sound, setting the stage for potential disaster next spring and summer.

The last time North Carolina's coast experienced so many damaging hurricanes was nearly 50 years ago, when four major storms visited our coastline in less than one year. Their names—Hazel, Connie, Diane and Ione—still elicit chilling memories among coastal residents and fishermen. Everyone hopes that we've seen our share of hurricanes—they have frayed our nerves and the state's economy. But if the climatologists are right, we have entered a new era of greater storm frequency and intensity.

Staggering flood recovery costs combined with these stormy forecasts are generating talk about how to make North Carolina's communities and environment more disaster-resistant. But this talk is unlikely to translate into meaningful actions unless we have good documentation of the extent and costs of the long-term environmental damage caused by the storm.

Right now virtually no funding is available for scientists to monitor Floyd's effects on water quality and fisheries. If they can't monitor what's happening, then the prospects are poor that lawmakers could enact effective programs to reduce the damage we may expect from future hurricanes.

Making believe we don't have a problem with water quality and fisheries habitat in North Carolina will only block the road to recovery. Only by understanding the linkages between landscape development and the health of our coast can we make wise decisions about the future.

Much that we have already done now seems unwise-building in floodplains, destroying wetlands and storing animal waste in open lagoons, particularly in areas subject to flooding. These practices expose our ecosystem and economy to undue risks. The hurricanes of '99 have sent us a clear message: clean up Pamlico Sound and our coastal rivers now!

Photo credit: Scott D. Taylor

Larry Crowder

Dr. Crowder's research centers on predation and food web interactions, mechanisms underlying recruitment variation in fishes, and on population modeling in conservation biology. He has studied food web processes in estuaries and lakes, and has used observational, experimental and modeling approaches to understand these interactions in an effort to improve fisheries management. He co-directed the South Atlantic Bight Recruitment Experiment (SABRE) and continues to conduct research on the life histories of estuarine-dependent fishes. He continues to conduct model and statistical analysis to assist in endangered species management for both aquatic (sea turtles) and terrestrial species (red-cockaded woodpeckers). Recently he has begun developing more extensive programs in marine conservation, including research on bycatch, nutrients and low oxygen, marine invasive species and integrated ecosystem management.

Todd Miller

Todd Lincoln Miller is the founder and Executive Director of the North Carolina Coastal Federation in Ocean, N.C. Founded in 1982, NCCF serves the 20 coastal counties and includes 5,000 individuals and 200 groups. It is the state's largest non-profit working to protect and restore the coast. Todd is a native of Carteret County in coastal North Carolina. He serves on several national steering committees including Restore America's Estuaries, Coast Alliance, Golf and the Environment and the Heinz Foundation Panel on Coastal Hazards. Todd holds a Master's degree in City and Regional Planning from the University of North Carolina at Chapel Hill.

Brushstrokes from Floyd

By

JoAnn M. Burkholder

A storm with one hundred forty mile-per-hour winds and a circumference the size of Texas was headed in a bull's-eye line straight for North Carolina...and a house surrounded by twelve large, shallow-rooted pines. In the already-pouring rain two days before, I'd packed four carloads of the possessions I care about most—pictures of my parents, my guitar, paintings mostly—and drove them to my office on the campus of NCSU. I'd just moved out of it; two days before Floyd passed through North Carolina, my laboratory had been in the midst of the final portion of a move that had taken, off and on, nearly four months to complete. My office had been the last of it. For thirteen years I had called a 10 ft x 20 ft little room on the fourth floor of an old, solid-as-a-rock brick building on the main campus "home." Two days before the hurricane, there was nothing left in it but an old desk and a computer. And a lot of space to move back into—at least, temporarily.

The room had had its moments, good and bad—like the times when I would hear a little sound and look down to find that a cockroach had fallen into my coffee; it had had its share of asbestos removal in the hallway, and mold caked on the ceiling panels; there were the big spiders I fought in a losing battle for years...but it didn't look bad, at all, for camping out during a hurricane the size of Floyd, making a straight-line approach to Raleigh. The room was ideal in that the only window faced another brick building, less than 20 feet away. A tree had managed to squeeze into the small space between the buildings. I hadn't considered it much of a view in the past, but during a hurricane, it offered a wonderful perspective from sheltered safety; a flock of robins had it figured about the same as I did. And the building itself was wonderfully solid, if cockroach-infested—it hadn't suffered any damage nor lost any power, even during Hurricane Fran.

We took some sleeping bags in and spent the night and early morning hours when Floyd passed by. My little dog hid under the desk. We shared the building with one other person of similar intent, passed him a couple of times in the halls. I'd spent many, many nights in the building with nobody there but an occasional policeman walking through, so it felt about the same except for the odd appearance of my office—loaded with artistry from home, the remaining space occupied by sleeping bags.

We turned off my computer, which we'd been using to continue to hit all of the weather websites, just before midnight and hoped for the best. I especially hoped I'd still have an intact house in the morning, considering what I'd heard about the approaching winds. For two days I'd enviously noticed my neighbor boarding up his windows; since I barely know which end of a hammer to use, and lacked his saws and other equipment, I decided if I tried such a thing it would bring more damage to my house than would leaving it alone.

The train-like roar of the winds was loudest at about 3:30 AM, but I slept through most of it, as I had Fran. The weather information had predicted that that was when Floyd would hit us, but an amazing thing happened just a few hours before the storm reached Raleigh...it veered to the northeast. My little dog and I were out at 7 AM, and it was a wonderful sight-just some branches down. We braved the roads a few minutes later and found only a few trees destroyed. Power was out in most of the city, déjà vu of Fran, but for the most part Raleigh had emerged extremely fortunate. Except for the power outage, most of the houses—including mine—were just fine.

We felt badly for those highlighted on the news whose houses had been in the way of the trees that were felled. The story of the big pine crashing right through the middle of what had been a nice home made me wince, since I had envisioned the same happening to my home, and had escaped that fate. The local newspaper was operating, but there wasn't a good update on the storm's consequences until the following day. By Friday we began to learn of the devastation in the eastern third of the state, but we considered that it was probably similar to what Fran had done...and then we heard that I-95 was flooded. The realization hit hard that we were 30 miles on the lucky side of another world. Floyd, unlike Fran, had missed us by a sliver...at least, as a direct hit.

Our new lab had a bit of mild flooding, with virtually no damage. The backup power generator, new and installed the day before Floyd passed, had kept our bio-hazard III *Pfiesteria* facility running without any loss of power—as compared with the nightmare scenario that had occurred after Fran, we had no worries about our cultures, or all of our research. But we'd been involved in an eight-year, intensive monitoring study of the Neuse River and Estuary, and we were very concerned about how the river, estuary and sound would be affected by the hurricane.

We had intensively monitored the Neuse after Bonnie, Bertha, Fran, and Dennis-double duty, in the latter case, when the storm turned and hit the state again. Fran's effects had been worst, with low oxygen throughout the water from surface to bottom of a 50-mile stretch, fish kills, high fecal bacteria, and high nutrient loading: impacts that had been obvious in our measurements for nearly two months, and more subtle for the following two years. We were anxious to get a boat out and sample right afterward to help the state health director and his staff determine the water quality from the perspective of human health protection, and to discover what had happened to the aquatic communities.

We sent a team from our lab out at 4 AM the following Monday, hoping to somehow get through and conduct a major sampling effort—and were turned back within 30 miles by the state highway patrol. We set out at 4 AM on Tuesday...with the same results. We waited two days and tried again, with no further progress. We scoured information services, called the Highway Patrol for updates, tried to take I-95 down to South Carolina and then loop back up...and were met with flooded roads and bridges.

Nearly a week later, we made it to Wilmington on the one road that was navigable. But we were unable to get a boat out the following frustrating week—at this point, nearly two weeks after the hurricane had passed. We obviously couldn't go under bridges, but as it turned out, we couldn't take a boat over them either, because the flooding was variable. The old saying, 'You can't get there from here,' was literally the truth...and it all began just 30 miles from Raleigh.

Working and waiting it out in the lab, we tried to picture what we were hearing, but we couldn't. How could the channel markers be completely underwater? How could Wilson literally be an island? How could a hotel in downtown Kinston be flooded up to three stories, or towns in the

Pamlico basin be completely submerged?

At one point we made arrangements with a helicopter and were about to get samples by suspended buckets from the helicopter, when we finally were allowed to get our boat onto part of the river and estuary. Even three weeks after the hurricane, though, we still had to use a small plane to fly our samples into a laboratory in Wilson that conducted the suite of fecal bacteria analyses we needed.

We viewed the flooded sewage treatment plant at Kinston with disgust; we felt badly for the people that would need that plant, and when we learned that it probably would not function well for several months, we felt badly for the Neuse ecosystem as well. We reacted with the fascinated, sinking feeling shared by many other people who saw the graphic photos of swine and poultry operations underwater. I personally felt very sorry for the people involved, and also sorry for the animals. Swine are intelligent and gentle-natured. When I was an adolescent, I saw the movie 'Bless the Beasts and the Children,' and the words of the theme song of that movie came to mind: 'For in this world they have no voice, they have no choice.'

It was sickening to see the swirls of purple sulfur bacteria moving straight into the Neuse from flooded animal waste lagoons; it was disgusting and sad to watch the effluent being sprayed onto waterlogged field that were above the floodline. There was no hope whatsoever that that effluent would be 'treated' by any absorption into the land. It was worse to learn that this had been a 150-year rainstorm that had caused a 500-year flood because of all of the changes that people, without thinking ahead, have caused to the eastern North Carolina landscape—all of the ditching, all of the impervious surface area, all of the wetlands destruction. Extreme rains like this had happened at least twice in the past few decades, and the flooding had not been nearly as bad.

I felt the most disgust in reaction to four post-Floyd occurrences. The first was when I repeatedly heard the statement that this was all just an 'act of God.' When it comes to human stupidity and lack of foresight, in my strong opinion, God or 'Mother Nature' get way too much credit. I think They'd just as soon pass on that and hold up a mirror for us to look into. We gave the devastating impacts of this storm a good boost of help. We're the developers who have fought to develop floodplains, as the recent post-hurricane debacle in Zebulon so sadly illustrates. We're the swine industry moguls who claim that our industry 'probably didn't contribute to any water quality problems because only a few swine lagoons burst'—conveniently forgetting, in our zealous propaganda to the newspapers, the operations that were completely flooded and so, were directly connected to our rivers: swine lagoons, dead bloating animals, and all. We're the well-intended people who ditched wetlands to farm better, back in the early to mid-1900s; we're the concerned people who shake our heads when we see the disgraceful, greedy actions of irresponsible developers translated into the loss of more than 9,000 acres of wetlands down by Wilmington—but don't say a word of protest to our legislators or bother to go to a meeting to demand that the wrong be righted. We are the people who seemed so surprised when we read the compelling quote released by the U.S. Weather Service: 'Within the past 25 years, more hurricane-level storms have passed within a 75-mile radius of Cape Hatteras than anywhere else on Earth.'

The second post-Floyd occurrence that disgusted me took place when I heard the following addition to that statement, "This was all just an act of God": "But don't worry, it won't happen again in our lifetimes." I guess that was the signal needed for the developers in Zebulon to justify continuing to build in floodplains. Maybe that was why the swine industry tried to convince our Congressional delegation that they should be allowed to rebuild in floodplains on taxpayer funds, while being exempted from cursory attempts to follow the Clean Water Act for six months or more.

This isn't the way to help the poor folks who own those operations, not in the long run or the short run either. We live in a state that has been struggling to find long-range vision to protect our natural resources—as evidenced by the piles of dead pigs from major swine operations in floodplains, and the completely flooded sewage treatment plants that will be out of commission for months. North Carolinians are not the only ones; this lack of vision is a disease that afflicts the nation.

Consider the massive Mississippi flood a few years ago. The worst flooding took place on the side of the river where the impervious area was greatest, and the concrete channelization existed...where there was literally nowhere else for the water to go but up. That flood was devastating. On the other side of the river, where there was still some area for the water to percolate and be absorbed by the earth, the flooding was much less.

The third post-Floyd situation that angered me was when I heard certain scientists begin to make efforts to cash in on the situation. I was contacted by many aquaculturists and fishermen who were extremely alarmed to hear that the Pamlico Sound had 'a dead zone that rivals the dead zone of the Gulf.' As I shook my head in disgust, I thought about the Gulf's dead zone. It comes from the huge Mississippi River, the biggest waterway in this country, and is the size of New Jersey in areal extent. Congress had discussed appropriating some funding for its study.

Shortly after my conversations with these individuals, I heard that scientists had launched a major effort to get millions of dollars in funding to study the nonexistent dead zone in Pamlico Sound. Researchers from our lab at NCSU went to about five times as many stations as did the scientists who had been granted funding. One week after they had sampled an area of the sound, we sampled that same area, as well as many others. Dissolved oxygen was plentiful from the surface to the bottom...yet the reports of the terrible 'dead zone' continued, to the New York Times, to Peter Jennings.

When we learned the basis for these scientists' claims, we were even more disgusted. According to their data, dissolved oxygen was depressed somewhat—but not badly, and only in the lower 3-6 feet (depending on the place sampled) of a 21-foot water column. Only six crabs had been reported dead. Not wanting to take the argument to the press, we quietly informed Division of Marine Fisheries staff and several other folks that no dead zone existed in the Pamlico Sound, and asked them to help get the word out.

In contrast to our response to the premature claims of certain scientists about the nonexistent dead zone, we were very direct with the many, many reporters who asked whether *Pfiesteria* would be much worse because of the hurricane. We repeatedly stated a clear, emphatic, 'NO, we don't believe so.' ·We explained that the hurricane's huge volume of water likely displaced a lot of the *Pfiesteria* population further down-estuary, into areas that are not as good for it to be encouraged to bloom. We pointed out that *Pfiesteria* activity, in general, has been lower than it was prior to Hurricanes Bertha and Fran. We stated that we were certain that there would be no *Pfiesteria* problem for the rest of 1999; and that we were hoping that 2000 would be a quiet year for *Pfiesteria*.

Some scientists reported a legitimate problem that we have been concerned about as well, and are working to understand—namely, the presence of a lot of diseased fish in the sound post-Floyd. Strong infusion of freshwater into previously salty conditions can stress fish and make them more susceptible to disease, as can various toxic materials. Floyd washed a witch's brew of these toxins into the estuaries and sounds. This is a problem that bears watching, as does the potential for more long-term prospects for algal blooms that may be stimulated by nutrient loading. Also, the rich organic milieu of raw sewage, animal wastes, and other materials into the estuaries and sounds may contribute to low-oxygen stress in the coming growing season.

Luckily, Floyd took place at a time of year when its impact on our aquatic resources will be minimized: the cold weather and winter storms may help to wash out some of the pollution before it can cause further harm. It would have been much worse, for sure, had this massive storm occurred in spring or summer.

The fourth frustrating post-Floyd event—the most hard-hitting of all—happened, as such events often do, when I least expected it. I had driven to Hickory in the western part of our state to give invited presentations on *Pfiesteria*, and on the serious problem of compromised science ethics in environmental issues. I'd used the pool, taken a nice hot shower and, while getting ready for a dinner engagement with professors of Lenoir-Rhyne College, turned on the local news.

The newscast turned out to be among the most high-impact, astute clips I had ever seen. The reporter was down in Pitt County, in Greenville. He described the people who were returning to homes that had been completely flooded, having lost most or all of their possessions; and then he paused and looked into the camera. What he said went something like this: "I can do a lot to convey the damage, and the sorrow of people who have lost so much. But what I can't convey to you is the smell." He held up a jar of Vaseline and explained that he had put some under his nose, but that it hadn't helped much.

The camera focused down on grass from some of the lawns of the flooded homes—grass that was coated with a brown substance. Then it quickly cut to a sign that said, 'For anyone who has walked on the grass, before you enter your homes, take off your shoes.' A health official had placed the sign there with the best of intentions, but I doubted that the message would make much of a difference—earlier photography had shown home after home where former living rooms had watermarks and brown material nearly up to the ceiling.

The camera then flashed to a health official who was being interviewed. He said, "This brown material on the grass has been tested. A lot of it is fecal material from human sewage and swine wastes." I stared at the image of a young couple standing on the street, looking at what had been their home, as a red 'X' indicating that it was condemned was sprayed onto the front door. I had tears in my eyes as I watched them silently cry. I heard about the people who died: the little boy who drowned trying to cross a road; the man who died trying to rescue some folks who were stranded; and many others. That newscast remained branded in my mind.

I hope that we become a little smarter at making tough decisions that require long-range vision. I hope that we can all pitch in and provide the massive funding, and the caring, that it will take to help the people down-east rebuild their lives. I really sympathize with the people of Princeville, whose town suffered terrible damage from Hurricane Floyd. Princeville is a wonderful historic town that was settled after the Civil War in a time when communities needed to be close to rivers in order to thrive. These waterways were the lifeblood of the countryside and the arteries of transportation.

We need to come to grips with the fact that our rivers and estuaries are, if anything, more than ever the 'lifeblood' of our state. An increasing number of people come here and, often without thinking, depend on them for potable water, for recreation, and for the beauty that they can and should offer. But, unlike in the immediate post-Civil War days, most of us don't need to build right next to them now. We have paved roads, cars, trucks, pipes, pumps...

I can understand the people of Princeville wanting to rebuild where they have rebuilt before, for all kinds of historical, sentimental, and spiritual reasons, strongly interwoven and locked within the past and present. But I don't have the same feelings for sewage treatment plants or concentrated animal operations, or new homes. We need to take better care of our remaining wetlands, the natural sponges of our watersheds that can absorb so much water—if we allow them to.

As I think of all of the devastation caused by Floyd that humans contributed to because of lack of foresight, and the potential impacts on our natural resources that may still be ahead, I realize that we need to take the protection of the health of our waters and our fish much more seriously. We need to get as much potentially pollution-contributing development out of our floodplains as possible—and we need to stop allowing more. We may not see another Floyd in our lifetimes—but we surely will see other severe floods, given our state's track record for hurricanes. Human beings need to use common sense, and invest a lot of effort, to help make sure that the next 25- or 50-year rainstorm doesn't cause a 100-year flood—for the sake of the people here now, the people who will follow us, and the natural resources upon which we, and they, must continue to depend.

JoAnn M. Burkholder

Dr. JoAnn M. Burkholder is a Professor of Aquatic Botany and Marine Sciences at North Carolina State University, and a Pew Fellow. She obtained a Bachelor of Science degree in zoology from Iowa State University, a Master of Science in aquatic botany from the University of Rhode Island, and a Ph.D. in botanical limnology from Michigan State University. Dr. Burkholder's research over the past 25 years has emphasized the nutritional ecology of algae, dinoflagellates, and seagrasses, especially the effects of nutrient pollution on algal blooms and seagrass disappearance. Since co-discovering the toxic dinoflagellate, *Pfiesteria piscicida*, in 1991, she has worked to characterize its complex life cycle and behavior, its stimulation by nutrient over-enrichment, and its chronic/sublethal as well as lethal impacts on commercially important finfish and shellfish in estuaries and aquaculture facilities. Aside from research and university-level teaching, she spends much of her time in environmental education outreach activities spanning age groups from first graders to adults. She also has worked to increase public recognition of a critical need for infusion of higher ethics, responsibility, and accountability among scientists in environmental issues. For her efforts in pioneering research on *Pfiesteria*, and in strengthening public under-standing of *Pfiesteria* and other water quality-related impacts on fish and human health, Dr. Burkholder has received many awards and honors, such as the 1998 Scientific Freedom and Responsibility Award from the American Association for the Advancement of Science, and the Conservationist of the Year Award from Governor Hunt and the North Carolina Wildlife Federation.

Flood Report: It's Time to Ante-Up

By

Rick Dove

I can imagine it now: Policy-makers sat hunched together on one side of the table, chuckling and protecting their hand. Opposite them sat Mother Nature who, with a finely arched brow, carefully watched them. This was a common occurrence, as the policy makers had taken to holding these poker games after hours around the state capitol—smoking fine cigars and drinking good liquor. The game never really ended, it just continued until the next time a "meeting" was called.

Mother Nature would always show up, and with a tolerant demeanor, usually pass on her turn. To them, her passing and silence was taken as a blessing to continue. Not once had they uttered the words "We Call." She, in her misplaced hope, simply continued to pass. So, they would take a careful look at their cards and then up the ante once again.

Sometimes it was to pipe their sewage and dump trash into her rivers and lakes. Sometimes it was to cut down her forest to create shopping malls and hotels with acres of concrete and asphalt. Then it was to fill in her wetlands so they could do something "useful" with the land. Finally, it was to build something called a lagoon where raw animal waste would sit until she could take care of it. I would imagine that the last one shocked her a bit, but not nearly so much as the next ante which would allow these 'waste pits' to be built in her floodplains, along with wastewater treatment plants, chemical companies, and junkyards.

At this the policy-makers must have felt some remorse, because they tried to console her with the bluff that rains causing enough flooding to impact these pits and plants only occurred every 500 years. What did they think? That she was born a mere half-century ago while they had been around for billions of years?

What her next move was, I'm not sure. Maybe she finally decided to call their bluff. Maybe she was protecting herself in a way that we could only hope to understand in generations to come. Maybe the extra tears of rain were for the many who suffered from the actions of the few who had gained. Whatever the case, it was time to ante-up.

Thursday, Sept. 16, 1999:

Today Hurricane Floyd hit the coast of North Carolina, leaving many residents confined to their homes and without power. Thankfully, Floyd had slowed to a weak category three before hitting our area, and by 4:00 p.m. his winds were a thing of the past. However, the effects of his rains would remain for weeks to come. Hurricane Floyd's 22 inches of rain combined with those left by Dennis to bring a total of 28 inches of rain to parts of eastern North Carolina.

As the winds abated, most people sat at home and gave a sigh of relief. They were unaware of the encroaching water that would soon endanger not only their homes and property, but their very health. Many people were caught so completely unaware that they had only minutes to pack up their most valued belongings. We're not sure how long it will take before it's safe for many of them to return home.

SEE NO EVIL, HEAR NO EVIL, SPEAK NO EVIL— We Broke All Three Rules:

As we plotted our course high above the Neuse River on the Friday following Floyd, what we saw in those two-and-a-half hours was the stuff of nightmares. We saw animal operations whose barns were almost completely covered with floodwater—a tragedy for the animals, the operators, and our environment. There were numerous large hog operations where flooding of barns and lagoons released visible plumes of waste into the surrounding waters.

As we continued to fly upstream, the number of farms with flooded barns and lagoons increased. Many farms would have one or more lagoons compromised, and other lagoons had as little as a foot to go before the waters reached them. In the Neuse Watershed alone, we counted around 25 lagoons that had been flooded. Fifty were within a few feet of being compromised.

Today, reports estimate that the number of lagoons compromised could reach as high as one hundred. Today the estimated number of hogs dead ranges from the industry's 15,000 to the media's 500,000. Poultry casualties are estimated in the millions.

Finally, we reached Kinston, and were even more disheartened by the sight of so many flooded homes and businesses and all the visible pollution. The Kinston wastewater treatment plants were failing and discharging untreated, human waste into the waters of the Neuse. Despite major efforts by the city following the sewer moratorium imposed by the state last year, repairs and upgrades did not occur in time to mitigate this event.

As we continued around Kinston, we saw numerous junkyards under water. Thousands of flooded cars and commercial businesses leached petroleum products into the surrounding waters. (Please remember that the Neuse River Foundation, working with the junkyard owners, has done much to try to halt the pollution of the Neuse that occurs when such areas flood.)

Let's 'Hear' What the Reporters Had To Say

From the *Raleigh News & Observer*:

Reporter James Shiffer wrote, "Beyond its toll in human lives, misery and property damage, the flooding of Floyd has plunged eastern North Carolina into an unprecedented environmental catastrophe." Reporters Shiffer, Wagner, and Shelman wrote, "Thousands of hog and poultry carcasses, animal waste from flooded farms, and oil slicks from washed out junkyards and warehouses are polluting eastern North Carolina, raising concerns about disease and drinking water safety." The *News and Observer* also quotes State Health Director Dr. Dennis McBride, who states, "A carcass is like a petri dish where things grow and are transported to people. We have to make sure we aggressively get to the livestock that is dead and get rid of them."

From the *New Bern Sun-Journal*:

Reporter Penny Round quotes Don Rueter, Public Affairs Director of DENR, who said, "You can't quantify it as just an environmental catastrophe, it's an economic catastrophe and a personal catastrophe for many people and there are significant environmental concerns, as well." In another article, Round writes, "At least 20 municipalities reported sewer plants that were flooded, overflowing, or discharging untreated sewage, and the floodwaters continue to rise."

From the Raleigh Associated Press:

In an article carried by the *Sun Journal*, the Raleigh Associated Press wrote the following: "People are fumbling with chainsaws, bees are swarming, and Hurricane Floyd's floodwaters are teeming with bacteria, sewage, and chemicals. The Press quoted Dr. Cathy Dover saying, "Now, especially due to the flooding, we are seeing more nausea and diarrhea, from drinking contaminated water, most likely."

From the *Winston-Salem Journal*:

In their Editorial section they wrote: "For more than a decade, while NC's swine population passed 9 million, state leaders knew they were gambling with environmental disaster. As the water from Floyd recedes, it is now clear that North Carolina just lost that bet. When legislators return to Raleigh next May, they should set a short-term deadline for the closing of all hog lagoons. This technology is not safe. Hurricane Floyd just proved that."

Let Us Speak Frankly of the Environmental Impacts of Floyd

Our immediate concern is the danger that polluted waters present to human lives. Raw animal waste (human, hog, and poultry) can contain harmful microbes such as *E. coli* and *Cryptosporretum*, which can cause diarrhea, fever, intestinal problems, and, occasionally, fatality. Hepatitis A can be contracted from food or water contaminated with human waste, and can cause liver malfunctions, chills, and fever. Tetanus can also be found in polluted waters, and symptoms of infection can progress from numbness to paralysis. In addition to these microbes, insects such as mosquitoes and blowflies can prove hazardous.

We are also focusing on the short and long-term effects of this pollution event on our beautiful river. Long-term effects include the addition of new toxins, sediments, and nutrients. This is a critical matter in view of the fact that the estuary was already suffering from an overload of these pollutants. Bear in mind that these pollutants will settle to the river bottom, but that does not mean they will remain there. The characteristics of the Neuse, which is shallow and highly receptive to wind currents, are such that the river bottom is frequently stirred, leading to the resuspension of settled pollutants to the water column.

Due to the nutrients and other pollutants discharged into our waters, which can lead to low dissolved oxygen, we also need to be watchful for fish kills. At this time we have already encountered measures of low dissolved oxygen and high levels of dangerous pathogens. So, a logical question would be: Are the fish safe to eat? State Health Director Dr. Dennis McBride has closely examined this matter and has concluded that the fish are safe to eat so long as they, like other foods, are properly prepared. We must also recognize that most North Carolina fishermen take pride in their work, and would not sell contaminated seafood.

Where Do We Go From Here?

The truth is, only the river knows how detrimental this pollution event will be to us environmentally and economically, and she'll tell us in due time. We can only hypothesize and wonder if we have the resources to cover the debt we now owe to Mother Nature. Let's hope that she is lenient in her collection, and that in her wisdom she allows all of us to learn from past mistakes. It's time to clean up our act and our waters. If given the opportunity, we should call off all old bets. And, if the game happens to be five-card draw, then let's hope the new policy makers are holding truth, integrity, honesty, concern, and the Ace—the courage to do what's right.

Downstream

By

Rick Dove

RAINY DAYS

In January, day after rainy day, I stared from my second-story office window overlooking a three-mile stretch of river and watched as downpours filled the Neuse. Trickles and gushers, again and again—would it ever end? When would the skies clear long enough for a bird's eye view of the river? The river was reported to be flooding, and that forecasted trouble for sewage treatment plants, hog facilities, farms, junkyards and other sources of pollution. We had witnessed pollution problems from these sources during the heavy rains of '96. Now, we would have to deal with them again. Was it bad? How bad? With that in mind, I could do nothing but suffer the torment of waiting for the rains to abate.

Then it happened—an excited call from Phil Bowie, our lead pilot, reporting an expected four-day clearing and a chance to fly. I remember Phil asking, "Are you ready?" It was Thursday, January 29th; my video batteries were overcharged; my camera bag was bulging with tape and film; and I had cabin fever. "Yes!" I said. "Gas up old Snoopy—I'll meet you in twenty minutes."

From the New Bern airport, takeoff was customarily smooth as Phil powered his Cessna into the air and up to a thousand feet in less than a minute. It was early morning and the air was calm. The flight would be steady. My stomach was thankful. The calm air also offered a great chance to shoot quality photos and video. Almost immediately the plane popped out over the Neuse and the worrisome display of bridge construction and a muddy river came into view. This time we could not see the discolored water typically caused by sediments being kicked up from the river's bottom by the big tugs and barges. The boats were working all right, but the river was so full of upstream sediments that we could not distinguish one source from the other.

This was bad, but not unexpected. These days the river is cursed by heavy sedimentation washing down from upstream cities like Raleigh, Cary, Morrisville and others during moderate and heavy rains. On this day the river looked more like the muddy Mississippi than it did the Neuse, and the shellfish lying on the river's bottom must have been suffering a terrible fate.

By this time both my cameras were in operation and recording events through an open window. When finished, I quickly closed the window to lock out those 100 mph winds that were draining my tear ducts. Then, without hesitation, Phil nosed Snoopy around to follow the river upstream to Kinston as we had planned. Along the way we could see that the Neuse was well over her banks.

When we arrived over Kinston, we could see a repeat of some of the devastating damage caused by the floods of '96. Kinston's Peachtree Waste Water Treatment Plant was surrounded by Neuse waters. It looked like a small island ready to be swamped. This was particularly alarming considering Kinston's poor environmental record for sewage treatment and maintenance at both of its treatment plants. We could also see that floodwaters were threatening houses and other buildings unsuitably located in the floodplain. The floodplain is part of the river and building anything in the river's path is senseless. Surely, the Neuse was communicating this point to all concerned.

As we glanced ahead, the first junkyard came into view. Cars by the hundreds, some under water up to their windshields, were discharging gas, oil, antifreeze and other dangerous pollutants. In '96, huge oil slicks could be seen flowing down the river from these junkyards. Back then we complained to state authorities, and they promised to do something—but here it was all over again.

As our flight along the Neuse approached Goldsboro, we observed more junked cars under water, and one small wastewater treatment plant located directly on the bank of the Neuse nearly overtaken by the floodwaters. The close-by Goldsboro sewage plant was also threatened.

After shooting what turned out to be some spectacular video footage, I heard Phil's voice squawking over the earphones: "Rick, you ready for hogs?" "Let's do it," I replied as I once again fought to close the window. Phil tipped the starboard wing and Snoopy gently circled back toward New Bern.

Crossing back and forth over the Neuse in a five-mile radius, we could see that the farm fields were saturated with water. But we were reassured by the crop farmers' inactivity. Surely, no farmer would waste his hard-earned money by applying fertilizer under conditions like these, where the chemicals would merely become river runoff.

While the farmers were being good stewards, some hog producers were not. In all, we observed approximately 15 incidents where hog waste was being improperly sprayed onto saturated fields.

After recording some of these polluting activities, Phil added power to Snoopy's single but faithful engine and speedily headed for home. After we shared all the video footage with the local TV stations, they aired a story on the evening news which focused on the flooding and was especially critical of hog producers. Hopefully, I thought, this would deter any more spraying until the fields dried.

The next day, Phil and I again flew the Neuse to Goldsboro. Overall, the situation had worsened. The river was still rising, and twice as many hog producers were spraying onto heavily ditched and sometimes barren fields saturated with water. In many incidents we could see the hog waste running into ditches leading directly to the river.

On our return to New Bern, I called state officials, as I had the day before, and reported what I had seen. Unfortunately, there were no hog inspectors on call, as they were all in Raleigh at a conference. The situation was like a bad dream, but that dream was about to turn into a real nightmare. That same evening as I watched the nightly news, I was alarmed to learn that a severe weather advisory, warning of flooding rains of more than three inches, was being issued for the coming Monday and Tuesday.

Fortunately, on Monday, we were able to fly before the rains started. This time Jane Ashford joined our crew to serve as a spotter. Jane, a Neuse River Foundation member and previous editor of the *Neuse River Notes*, had never flown in a small plane before; but, she professed to have a strong stomach and her assistance was greatly needed. Nevertheless, I did locate the airsickness bags just in case.

As we took off, we were all amazed that the weather was clear and the air smooth. By now all weather forecasters were predicting, with certainty, the arrival of a severe storm later in the day. Before it was over, between three and seven inches of rain were expected to flood the coastal landscape. Since the improper spraying of hog waste was now our main concern, this is where we concentrated our effort.

Jane was doing well, except for her cries of "no tippee tippee." You see, to turn the airplane you dip a wing. No dipping, no turning—it's that simple. After we explained to Jane that we didn't have enough fuel to circle the globe, she accepted the inevitable and began to prove herself a real trooper and a great spotter.

Then the horror struck! Hog producers were spraying everywhere. One, and another, again and again—we couldn't believe our eyes. By all estimates, seventy percent of the facilities we observed were disregarding the forecast of heavy rains and dumping animal waste, loaded with dangerous pathogens and nutrients, onto heavily ditched fields still saturated with water. In the five years I have served as Riverkeeper, I recall nothing that has concerned and angered me more. I began to think about those expensive hog commercials and how they were so misleading. My mind flashed back to images of wetlands, streams and creeks covered with algae, *Pfiesteria*, fish with sores and millions upon millions of dead fish. It was a sickening sight and I thought it fortunate that I knew where the airsickness bags were located.

While landing, we saw another disturbing sight. Craven County was spraying human waste onto fields adjacent to the runway. While this waste, unlike hog waste, is disinfected before spraying, it is still loaded with nutrients that would be washed into the river by the heavy rains. It was a terrible way to end the flight, but I had little time to dwell on the matter. It was getting late and little time was left to share the information with the public through the media.

Fortunately, there was just enough time for staff from two area TV stations to accompany me to a local hog facility located on the Trent River that was still spraying hog waste. On the segment, which aired that night, I noted that with flooding rains expected in hours, the nutrients then being applied, especially nitrogen, would be washed into the river. In response, the operator, who is also a livestock industry official, remarked that the nitrogen being applied to the field would be taken up by the crop and that it would not run off to the river because it had no way of coming up out of the ground. Of course, that was nonsense and the inappropriateness of that statement was confirmed by a number of officials and scientists who were later contacted.

Yes, the storm hit with a vengeance and we got all of what was predicted. Some say it could have been worse—but I don't know how. After sharing our experience with state officials, I was dismayed to learn that while wastewater treatment plants had reported discharging untreated waste, not one hog producer had reported a discharge to surface waters. I wonder where they think it all went?

Rick Dove

As spokesperson for the Neuse River, the Riverkeeper has appeared in more than 4,000 news stories over the past seven years. Media coverage includes CNN, NBC, CBS, ABC, CBN, NPR, BBC, and many local TV and radio stations in North Carolina, Virginia, Iowa, Kentucky, Florida, Georgia and Maryland. Some of his national publications include: *The New York Times*, *Sports Illustrated*, *Health* magazine, *Natural History*, *George* magazine and *The Washington Post*. One chapter of the book, *And the Waters Turned to Blood*, (Simon and Schuster, published 1997) details Rick Dove's work on the Neuse River related to the microorganism *Pfiesteria*.

Did We Create Our Own Flood Crisis in Eastern North Carolina?

By

Stanley R. Riggs

In September 1999, eastern North Carolina faced torrential rains and extreme floods. The "flood of the century" resulted from several major factors. First, the flood was a product of two back-to-back hurricanes that made landfall on North Carolina's coastal plain. Hurricane Dennis dropped up to ten inches of rain in early September and put the major rivers well above flood stage by the time Hurricane Floyd followed two weeks later and dumped up to twenty inches of rain over the same general area. However, additional factors were also responsible for the extreme consequences of these storms.

From the 1960s to early 1990s, eastern North Carolina experienced extensive growth and development but had only a few minor hurricanes. The resulting urban sprawl converted vast areas of forest and agricultural land to paved surfaces and lawns, significantly increasing stormwater runoff that in turn increased frequency and magnitude of flash flooding. The cumulative impact of this growth and development severely modified the region's drainage systems. Many tributary streams throughout eastern North Carolina were extensively channelized, and adjacent marginal uplands and associated wetlands were ditched and drained. These drainage programs were designed to remove surface water from marginal lands quickly and efficiently for alternate uses including agribusiness, forestry, industry and low-cost housing. During heavy rainfalls, greater volumes of water are quickly 'piped' downstream by these channeled tributaries, aggravating flood conditions in the main trunk stream. In addition, expansion of the highway system resulted in many roads being constructed on fill material across floodplains with minimal-sized culvert and bridge openings over the main channels. The resulting 'road dams' significantly diminish floodplain flow when rivers and streams are in flood stage. This causes floodwaters to back up, often exacerbating upstream flood conditions, and to ultimately blow out the roadbeds when they are finally overtopped. Moving floodwaters through channelized streams or holding back floodwaters with road dams might locally aid in diminishing flood impacts from small storms. However, the magnitude of stream alteration and our subsequent migration into and encroachment upon these changed drainage systems resulted in the catastrophic impacts of the 1999 floods.

Prior to this period of rapid growth and drainage modification, similar storm events resulted in significantly smaller floods. In fact, larger hurricanes often didn't even produce record floods. For example, six major hurricanes crossed the North Carolina coastal plain between August 30 and October 15 of 1954 and from August 12 to September 20 of 1955 and brought unprecedented destruction (Hurricanes Carol, Edna, and Hazel in 1954 and Connie, Diane, and Ione in 1955). According to the National Weather Service, the first two storms of 1955 dropped up to 30 inches of rain on portions of the central coastal plain, with another 16 inches falling on the same area during the third storm. The press reported unprecedented rainfall that led to heavy runoff with floodwaters inundating vast areas of eastern North Carolina. However, river flood levels in 1955 only reached 23.5 feet in Tarboro and 17 feet in Greenville, as compared to the previous flood record of 34 feet and 24.5 feet in 1919, and the new flood record in 1999 of 38 feet and 30 feet, respectively. Why?

A river is a drainage system designed to carry surface water off the land and back to the oceans by gravity. Rivers have many parts, including the main channel that carries the day-to-day water flow, the primary floodplain that carries the increased river volume during the rainy season and other small storms, and the secondary floodplain that carries high water volumes resulting from very large storm events. The primary floodplain consists of wetlands dominated by special vegetation that filters the water and holds it like a sponge for slow release, and thus maintains a more uniform river flow throughout the year. The channel and primary floodplain should not be violated under any conditions.

The secondary floodplain is used much less frequently by rivers and may not consist of obvious wetland vegetation; however, when a river needs this floodplain it will reoccupy it. We can share the latter floodplain, but it must be done on the river's terms or there will be a catastrophe. Should we allow drainage systems to be re-engineered by specific user groups that jeopardize the natural function of the system? Should short-term economic pressures allow the heart of a modern city (sewage lines, sewage and water treatment plants, and power substations), as well as housing and industrial facilities to be built within these secondary floodplains that will always be marginal lands for development?

Since most communities actively pursue an expanding growth mode, it is more important than ever for society to understand how the most basic resource (water) works on our finite planet. Rivers operate within a natural set of rules. Communities intimately tied to and dependent upon river systems must understand and respect these rules; to ignore them is a negligent act that ultimately ends in disaster.

Have we created our own crisis in eastern North Carolina through the systematic and traumatic modification of our watersheds during the last several decades? Can—and will—it happen again if we continue to modify and encroach upon riverine systems? Yes, and it probably won't take 100 years, or even 500 years, as many believe. Rather, it is like rolling dice: the 100-year or 500-year flood could be rolled again next year, or anytime in the near future. Thus, rebuilding must be based upon our scientific understanding of river systems and this knowledge utilized in planning all future growth and development. Locations of the 100- and 500-year floodlines change with time as we modify the character of drainage systems and must be regularly upgraded to be meaningful. And most importantly, we must begin to restore the natural drainage systems, move our infrastructure out of the floodplains, and prevent further political and economic migration into these marginal lands. To do otherwise guarantees frequent repeat performances of the tragedy that we have just experienced.

Stanley R. Riggs

Dr. Riggs is a Distinguished Research Professor in the Department of Geology at East Carolina University. He is a coastal and marine sedimentologist and stratigrapher who has been doing research on modern coastal systems since 1964. His area of research extends from the inland riverine and lacustrine environments, to the estuarine and barrier island systems, and seaward across the continental shelf. His areas of interest lie in sedimentation, Quaternary and Tertiary stratigraphy, coastal and mineral resources, and their inter-relationship with the development of human civilization. Dr. Riggs has been actively involved in numerous technical coastal and mineral resource issues at the Federal, State, and local levels which has included appointments to many commissions, task forces, panels, and committees. These appointments, as well as many of his publications, have dealt directly with integrating scientific understanding and utilization and management of various coastal systems including such critical issues as shoreline erosion, hazard zone delineation, utilization of mineral resources, inlet dynamics, water quality, and habitat preservation.

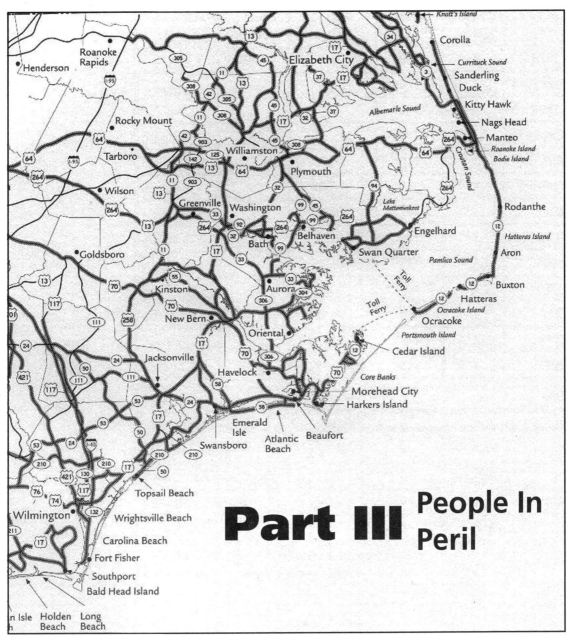

Part III People In Peril

Hurricane Evacuation Routes. Source: N.C. Division of Emergency Management

Hurricane Home, Carolina

By

E. W. Zrudlo

Hurricane Fran initiated us into the world of hurricanes. Bonnie dropped a tree on our place. Dennis sent us scurrying. Floyd blew us up I-40 and made us wonder if we'd ever return, then if we'd survive. And Irene, dear Irene, simply confirmed where we live—in the Carolina climate of Wilmington, far from our former home: wintery Canadian Ottawa.

When Bonnie pushed an oak tree onto our roof, it seemed a reasonable occasion to reconsider the lease on a dwelling seventeen miles from the beach. Fran's residential demolition had forced us to an area we did not know existed, and Bonnie's less-than-gentle rapping pointed us back to our original destination, Carolina Beach. If hurricanes knocked us about inland, what did it matter if we lived at the beach? We moved into a ground-level cottage that had weathered everything that blew off the Atlantic for fifty years, and enjoyed the shade of water oaks, a willow tree, and our neighbors' houses sitting twelve feet in the air on big stilts. Let the neighbors walk up and down all those stairs; we'd walk the beach.

Then came Dennis. After Fran and Bonnie, everyone paid attention right from the time it reached tropical storm strength. I stopped at the ABC store every day to collect a few sturdy boxes which I broke down and stored behind the couch. I bought big roles of cellotape. I borrowed a friend's utility trailer to move our key pieces of furniture. I bought tarps. I had everything under control.

Beverly, my wife, went to visit friends on Ocracoke Island. She'd be back in time, she said. Meanwhile, Dennis swerved, strengthened and speeded up. I drove the utility trailer onto the lawn and up to the door, grabbed a neighbor, and lugged out the furniture. The rain started before I got the tarps tied down.

A swarm of neighbors appeared. "You've got to get out," they said. "What can we do?" I pulled the boxes out from behind the couch. Knicknacks, ornaments, photos, books—"You sure got a lot of books"—disappeared, unlabeled, into innumerable bright-colored liquor boxes. "Where do they go?"

Good question. I might have gathered all the hurricane supplies, but my wife is the organized one. The neighbors sensed this. "Where's Beverly?" they inquired. I mentioned Ocracoke. "What! She'll never make it back. The ferries are closed." Oh dear.

Our neighbor Marsha took charge. "We'll put the boxes in your camper. Is it working?" It was—sort of. The engine and the brakes functioned, but nothing else did, courtesy of Hurricane Fran. I was attempting to restore it. Into the camper went all the boxes. I hoped there'd be time to deal with the problem of two vehicles and one driver. Back in the house, we assembled milk crate columns in the middle of the bedrooms to support sheets of plywood. We piled the rest of the furniture and the clothes from the closets on these makeshift tables.

Beverly drove up in our battered white Volvo. She'd just managed to get on the last ferry. It was hard to say whose relief was greatest—mine, hers, or the neighbors.' But now we had three vehicles and two drivers.

The closer Dennis got, the harder it rained. I dragged out the car dolly from the backyard. The car could go on it and be towed by the camper. I hoped the dolly's lights worked.

Turned out that most of them did, but the all-important swivel did not. Unless the car could swivel to take the turns, the thing was useless.

I picked up my sledgehammer and swung it in an insane imitation of Hephaestus, the Greek god of smiths, hoping to break the seal of rust and corrosion. The wind had risen high enough that I scarcely heard a sound of steel pounding steel, my mind willing the blows to fall as fast as the rain. Somehow everything managed to get done and we drove away to the final evacuation warning.

A few miles down the road the swivel seized up again. Whenever I drove over forty, the car swayed behind me like the tail of a vicious cat. Everyone kept their distance.

We drove thirty miles inland to Riegelwood, where we'd ridden out Hurricane Bonnie with our friends Tim and Mary. We had arrived early enough during Bonnie to watch the stinging rain shift from vertical to horizontal. Seven of us stayed there that time, as well as three dogs and four cats. Our two cats sat up all night with my wife and stared out the unshuttered patio doors that pulsated to the heartbeat of the hurricane, moving in and out like a glass diaphragm until Beverly feared they would shatter. I recall missing her in the bed and getting up to find her sitting there on the floor, a Siamese cat on either side of her, all staring out into the storm.

When Bonnie stalled over Wilmington and no end could be reasonably predicted, we decided to take the dogs out to see if they'd do their business. We should have known that when you have to carry ordinarily active dogs outside, there will be a problem. The two older and bigger ones quickly found the lee of the house. My puppy simply blew away. What did I know about hurricanes and puppies? I chased the bundle of wet fur over twenty feet before I caught her. She still shivers when hurricanes blow in.

When we returned home after Bonnie, it seemed as though we had just got the furniture off the plywood tables when news of Floyd screamed at us. Maybe it would be like Dennis—a great deal of anxiety and then a great deal of relief. We could handle that. As Floyd grew, though, spread its spinning arms ever wider, and swelled past a category three to a category four and then to a dreaded five, we felt the fear of impending obliteration.

The utility trailer was pressed back into service and hauled a huge load of furniture to a hastily rented storage unit. Our twenty-year-old daughter had just returned from a summer away. Without her young muscle I could not have shifted so much stuff in such short order. Always encourage daughters to play rugby if you live in a hurricane zone—the training's invaluable. And make sure they have boyfriends who, while they wait for your daughter's flight, also move furniture.

What did not go into storage went into the camper—kitchen furniture, TV, stereo, all our clothes, dishes, files, and whatever was loose. The books were still in there. Our camper's capacity impressed me. The plywood tables with their milk crate columns reared up like mushrooms. I drove our wheezing little pick-up and the utility trailer to the highest ground on Carolina Beach, a neighbor's driveway. I wished them well and left, not noticing the cab light glowing dimly. The car dolly remained in rusty disgrace under a myrtle.

During this last flurry of activity, we had dispensed with our rain gear. What was the point? It was ninety degrees. We rushed around in bathing suits and T-shirts, the perspiration of our anxiety matching the precipitation of the hurricane.

With full gas tanks and a pocketful of dollars siphoned from a reluctant ATM, we headed for the hundred-mile parking lot that, the day before, had been a high-speed interstate leading to Raleigh. Six hours later we pulled into a gas station just west of I-95, my wife and I in the camper and our daughter following in the car.

Beverly opened a can of stew, but the camper stove didn't work. During the drive, she had changed into a simple dress made shapeless by crushing and dampness. She'd lost her shoes somewhere in the camper. She walked shoeless into the gas station with a bowl of cold stew to beg the use of a microwave, and came back laughing as she described the looks the attendants gave her. The stew was hot, though.

Back onto the I-40 parking lot. Three hours later, we gave up trying to get anywhere and pulled into The Flying J truck plaza. Surely such a place would be safe from the ferocious winds predicted by excitable meteorologists. Although no one could give us the genesis of its name, it proved to be an oasis, complete with a laundromat, TV lounges, snacks at grocery store prices, and truckers, the only people who seemed to know anything about what was going on. We rearranged some boxes and furniture in the camper and made space enough to sleep. My dog had stopped shivering.

The next day dawned beautiful and clear. Had Floyd been real?

"Where's your stove?" Beverly asked.

"The WhisperLite?"

She nodded.

"In the car somewhere. Why?"

She handed me bacon, eggs, and diced potatoes. "You and Erika are making breakfast, that's why. But boil some water for coffee first."

There in the RV parking lot of The Flying J, Erika and I did what we'd done on dozens of Adirondacks hikes and Canadian canoe trips. In the warmth of the morning sun, we cooked a brilliant breakfast on a one-burner stove.

Floyd, of course, fell to a category three before it made landfall and then skirted the coast, dropping a great deal of rain but delivering no devastating winds. We stayed one more day at The Flying J and then started for home—we thought. At I-95 signs declared every road to Wilmington closed. No state troopers or soldiers enforced the signs. They were obviously out of date. The hurricane was over. We drove on-for twenty miles. At that point, troopers and soldiers directed all vehicles off I-40. And no, they did not know what route to Wilmington was open.

Every route magically seemed to lead to Newton Grove, which sported a traffic circle in the middle of its tiny existence. A Piggly Wiggly grocery was situated to the north of it, a Hardee's to the west, an Exxon station to the south, and an abandoned building to the east.

First we spun east. Ten miles later, the lakes newly formed from hurricane rains and rising creeks had swallowed the road and forced us back. Another spin. We whipped to the south and into another lake. Back to the fairy traffic ring. We looked for a wizard to ask us a riddle whose correct answer would save us and spun north to Wilson, which was fast becoming an island in the midst of rising rivers. The traffic circle again, frustrating parody of too many hurricanes. West and back to I-95. Where were Dorothy's ruby slippers when we needed them?

Another truck plaza, but no memorable name this time and fewer amenities. Not all plazas are created equal. Stories of truckers trapped further north, of vehicles washed away on bridges, of people swept away when they got out their cars stalled in water. Contradictory information about routes into Wilmington. Unclear information about damage. We couldn't go home, if we still had one, and no one knew where we were except relatives a thousand miles away.

Military helicopters menaced the sky ineffectually. Fleets of electric repair trucks flooded the truck plaza. We counted over fifty trucks in one convoy and CP&L paid the restaurant tab for over a hundred men. I discovered a town, Dunn, and bought a new auxiliary battery for the camper. When I connected it, I realized that the old one had been connected backwards. The new one gave us lights for twenty minutes, then died. In a hurricane, does it matter which way an auxiliary battery is connected?

Days passed. We had been cast in a play of the absurd. Where was Godot anyway?

Then my daughter made contact with a friend who lived near Wilmington. Route 211 was open. At least, it had been. The friend had driven home on it. We filled the gas tanks, raced down I-95, turned onto the two-lane 211, and rocketed along it at interstate speeds. The camper took up the whole right lane. It swayed like a demented elephant. Water lapped the road at every bridge. None of the rivers had crested yet. Fallen trees had pulled down power lines. Dead livestock floated in swollen ditches. Suddenly a detour, then another. A flock of African guinea fowl wandering the side of the road. Had the hurricane blown them over?

And then we were at Highway 17, a four-lane divided highway. Although it led to Wilmington, we couldn't go there because of the flooding. But we could make it to Oak Island, the spot hardest hit by the hurricane.

We had stopped trying to make sense of anything back in Newton Grove's traffic circle. Erika's friend lived on Oak Island, so we drove there, parked in his driveway, and showered in his bathroom. What else was there to do?

The next day I drove to Carolina Beach in the car, the only one of our vehicles with a resident's sticker on the windshield. I scarcely noticed my route, choosing to flow in a Zen state of mind. Traffic conditions responded in a positive sort of way—I don't recall a single red traffic light. No National Guardsmen blocked my way over Snow's Cut Bridge from where I saw my Carolina sea again at last. The only soldier I met stopped me as I turned to go to the north end of the island where I lived. We chatted briefly. "Good luck!" he said, and waved me through.

The beach covered the main road. If the drifts had been white, I would have nodded familiarly at a blizzard's snowy remains. But they were piles of sand—tons of it-that the hurricane had deposited to mock bulldozers, loaders and dump trucks. Mountains of trash—ruined appliances, furniture, carpeting, clothing, lawnmowers, bicycles—rose from the bottoms of stairs and the ends of driveways.

When I pulled into my driveway, not even the few inches of water that covered it and my yard could squelch my thankfulness. Our house still existed. We had most of our possessions. I walked in. So what if the appliances were dead, the carpeting ruined and the floors broken?

"Welcome back!" called a neighbor. He walked in. "The water only went up to the bottom of the windows."

"Could've been worse," I volunteered.

All of our neighbors had returned the next day. They were mostly tidied up and ready to help us. First I had to call Beverly and tell her to come back. After she heard my description, she decided to wait a day. I would stay and start the cleanup. Our friend Bill outfitted me with clean clothes after I showered at his place after a day's work. The shirt said I was a member of the Jimmy Buffet Parrothead Club. Margaritaville never sounded so good.

Marsha, who had been so helpful when we were evacuating for Dennis, said I could sleep at her house. She was worried about looters anyway, she said. Right. She owned a Rhodesian Ridge-back.

Marsha called her husband, who was in Texas on a job. She said if any of the neighbors ever said anything about a strange man in her house, he was to know it was only me. Then she got out her new queen-size air mattress. Did I know how to work it? she asked. Yeah, yeah, no trouble. She brought out sheets and a down comforter in case I got cold.

Her laughter woke me up the next morning. "What happened?" she wanted to know. I lay in a heap of sheets, comforter, Rhodesian Ridgeback and a completely deflated mattress. "I think there's something wrong with the plug," I confessed.

She rooted in the mattress box and held up a solid rubber plug, the one you put over the hole before you screw on the cap. "I thought you said you knew what you were doing?"

"I do. It's just that ... well, I'm suffering from hurricane stress." How easily the excuse came. She didn't look convinced. Her husband is an engineer.

Flotsam still covered our yard when we started hearing about Hurricane Irene. Three in one month? We were still camped out in our driveway, making treks to the bathroom, which mercifully worked. The floors were being repaired, mold grew daily on the walls, a few shingles needed replac-ing, screens demanded attention. Leave again or stay, that was the question. Hamlet got it wrong.

"What do you think?" someone asked Bill one afternoon when a group of us idled in his driveway.

"I think it's a pretty fine day, that's what I think."

We all looked into a flawless blue sky and nodded. There was no denying that Carolina sky. Besides, if we did go, we'd only reach the traffic circle in Newton Grove and be flung back. I secretly clicked the heels of my flip-flops and repeated the mantra: There's no place like home.

Photo credit: Beverly Zrudlo

Ted Zrudlo

E.W. Zrudlo moved to the Wilmington area from Ottawa, Canada four years ago. Escape from Winter was the reason, everyone thought. And in part it was. But there was also Escape To. Both Ted and his wife are travelers and, after raising their family in Ottawa, needed to get moving again. They moved to Wilmington, N.C., where Ted teaches at Cape Fear Academy and UNCW. He writes poetry and humorous commentaries on everyday life. He has published two ESL texts. After living most of his life in Canada and Europe, he is finding his extended stay in Carolina a bigger adventure than he had a reasonable right to expect.

Hurricane Hangover

By

Nan Graham

The adrenaline rush that always accompanies hurricane warnings was definitely there on Sunday. By that afternoon our houseguests had left, the cars were gassed, batteries ready, food and water on hand. Lugging the last outsized terracotta pot of geraniums and the rusty metal dragonfly from the front lawn, we collapsed with fatigue.

Hurricane Dennis was due late tomorrow, according to the storm gurus. About one o'clock Monday morning, it was evident that impatient Dennis was on our doorstep: the wind whistled, we were pelted with driving rain, and lightning illuminated the sky. Then our power failed—always a particularly bad phenomenon for our little dead-end street, since it means no lights or water. We all have wells, and our well pumps run on electricity. All of our water comes from our well: drinking water, sink water, bath water, and, most crucially...toilet water. Our inability to flush became alarming as the dark hours ticked by.

We are only a block from the Intercoastal Waterway and have inherited an antiquated electric line that has a history of always-and I do mean always—being the last power line in New Hanover County to be repaired. Our neighborhood is part of the city now, although we do not have city water. We've recently been annexed, so we're supposedly better off than we were before. Mind you, we are not in the hinterlands. But, like a wallflower at a dance, our street is always the last to be asked to rejoin the "body electric," to quote Walt Whitman.

Frustrated, I called WHQR, our public radio station, to see if they had a telephone number that might connect me with a human being. My calls to the electric company had all been answered by automatic metallic voices grimly reassuring me that our problem had been "duly noted."

About an hour later, the phone rang. My husband answered it, and when he hung up he told me that a team from National Public Radio was coming over to interview us. We were among the few families in New Hanover County who didn't have electricity, and the media was desperate for material. The hurricane had underwhelmed everybody, and had made for dreary copy. Our power-less world with flushing problems must have been the ultimate non-story.

I threw on some lipstick. (My daughter says this habit is so "fifties," but in lipstick I feel like I'm ready for my close-ups...even on the radio.) I also stuck on some red Chinese earrings. Not until I was ushering in the media folk did I realize that I was barefoot. I hoped I looked wonderfully eccentric.

The interviewers were great. They seemed to like my Hurricane Fran story about our eight-day aftermath when we had to go to Hardee's, two blocks away, to brush our teeth, wash our faces, and meet other needs. Even on my best days, I've never been one for the camping life. A week of living out of a public bathroom is difficult for me to classify as an adventure.

I never heard this interview on NPR, but I'm not bitter about not making the cut...because today we have electricity, and are flushed with excitement.

Floyd and the Chainsaw Chicken

By

Nan Graham

We knew from the weather reports that Hurricane Floyd was likely to be the real thing, baby. This hurricane we were going to evacuate to Goldsboro, to a local motel. Here's the rationale: it's only ninety miles away, an hour-and-a-half ride. Also, it's my husband's hometown, and though he hasn't lived there in forty years, it promised that reassuring cushion of familiarity.

Arriving too early for check-in, my husband and I drove around. He pointed out the landmarks: "There's the old Goldsboro High School. Did you know that Andy Griffith used to teach drama there? And there's where Cuttin' India's house was, next to Mawmaw's. Did you know that..."

Suddenly, hurricane nerves kicked in. Did I know? Did I know? I was not exactly his date. I have been married to this man for more than thirty-eight years and even lived in Goldsboro for fourteen months myself when he was in Vietnam. We drove on without the nostalgic litany.

That night, ensconced in our motel, we heard the rain and wind howl. We were starving from our frenzied evacuation, and were glad there was a restaurant in the building so we didn't have to brave the weather. Called the Crossroads Country Café, the restaurant featured an extensive buffet of country delectables, according to the sign in the lobby—and for only $4.25 including beverage!

As we entered the doorway of the dining room, an enormous eight-foot-tall creature loomed over us. It was an amazing sight: a giant chicken—a rooster, to be exact. The animal was white, with a red comb and chrome-yellow beak and feet. The scale of the wooden sculpture was impressive.

On close inspection, I recognized the features of the bird. It was Foghorn Leghorn, the character from the cartoons of yesteryear. You remember, the one with the distinctive Southern accent: "A real Southerner, boy...Deep South, that is."

The hostess told me that the artist was a local who lived out on Highway 117 and had carved the remarkable bird with a chainsaw from a single log, except for the three tail feathers, which had been carved separately and inserted at a jaunty angle.

"Is it the Leghorn chicken character from the cartoons?" I asked.

"Well, yeah, but"—she leaned in confidentially—"we all call him Earl."

The sculpture was an *objet d'art* with a practical purpose. Tucked under one wing, a chalked message on school slate read, "Hey. Come on in and have a seat." So we did.

The buffet was as remarkable as the giant chicken. Hot biscuits, cornbread, tiny field peas and snaps, white corn cut from the cob, string beans, squash, sliced tomatoes and cukes, huge trays of red jello with all sorts of fruit cut up in it, and the requisite Southern dessert, homemade banana pudding.

The meat was another thing: fried chicken, cut by someone with no knowledge of the bird's anatomy. Even Earl would have had problems recognizing a cousin. Then came the pork offerings. I had difficulty identifying most: chitlins, lean strips pulled from the ham hock, hog jowls, and large chunks of "the other white meat" with what looked like lard on them. I decided to go vegetarian.

We were sad to leave Earl, the magnificent giant chicken, after our breakfast the next morning. Our evacuation destination had been a successful choice: we never lost power, the food was hot and plentiful, and Earl's hurricane hospitality was hard to beat. He never lost the smile on his beak.

Now, getting home was another story.

Nan Graham

Nan Graham, born in Tallahassee, Florida, graduated from the University of North Carolina at Chapel Hill with an B.A. in English. She received her MAT in English from the Citadel in Charleston, South Carolina, decades before the first female Citadel cadet arrived.

She is currently teaching composition and literature at the University of North Carolina at Wilmington where she has been a lecturer for the past ten years. She has also taught at Cape Fear Community College and at the Citadel.

The recipient of a Sarah Graham Kenan award, she compiled and published a directory for post secondary education in North Carolina, a comprehensive study of facilities available for learning disabled and dyslexic students. A bi-weekly commentator for the local public broadcasting station WHQR, her familiar sign-off line is: "Commentator Nan Graham is a life-long Southerner."

At this time she is compiling a collection of her nonfiction essays selected from her five years on air. Also the co-author of a novel set in the Depression in the mountains of North Carolina, she is working on what she hopes will be the final revision.

Nan lives in Wilmington with her husband, a West Highland Terrier, and a semi-feral cat named Sumter.

What They Don't Tell You About Hurricanes

By

Philip Gerard

What they don't tell you about hurricanes is the uncertainty.

First it's whether. As in Weather Channel. There's been a rumor of a storm off the coast of Africa, and it's turned into a tropical depression. It churns across the Atlantic into the Caribbean and is upgraded to a Tropical Storm, winds at forty or fifty knots, and the person in charge of such things gives it an androgynous name: Fran.

Will it hit us here on the south coast of North Carolina?

They can't tell. The experts. We've been through this before—Hugo, Felix, Marilyn, Edouard, Bertha. My wife Kathleen, who grew up with California earthquakes, bridles at the lingering uncertainty, the waffling, a whole season of emergency. She wants it quick, bang, and over. But it doesn't happen that way. Hurricanes are big and slow and cyclone around offshore for a few thousand miles.

So the radar scope on the Weather Channel becomes familiar, part of the nightly ritual before going to bed, like taking out the dog and locking the front door. It becomes the first thing you do every morning, even before coffee. Watching the swirls of red and orange, a bright pinwheel of destruction. Checking the stats—wind speed, barometric pressure, latitude and longitude. We are at 34 degrees 12 minutes north latitude, 77 degrees 50 minutes west longitude. A degree of latitude equals sixty miles north or south. The arithmetic isn't hard.

* * *

Fran bangs into some islands from the vacation brochures and it's heading toward the U.S. mainland. But here in Wilmington, we just had Bertha, a direct hit. The eye sat over our backyard— you could look up and see the actual sky wound into a circular wall, like being down inside a black well, watching the stars out the top.

Surely, not twice in one season—what are the odds?

What they don't tell you is that hurricanes, like lightning, can strike exactly the same spot time and again. Fran is not the first storm. It's the second slam from a hurricane in eight weeks, and in the meantime it's rained torrentially almost every day. It's been a whole summer of violent storms, of lightning fires and local floods, of black line squalls that knock down fleets of sailboats racing off the beach. The ground is so saturated we have had the lawn sprinkler system turned off all summer. Starved of oxygen, tree roots are rotting in the ground.

The longleaf pines that ring our property stand sixty and seventy feet high, two feet in diameter, precarious upright tons of wet wood, swaying already in the breeze. Their roots are soft in the spongy ground.

We've been set up. It feels like there's a bull's-eye painted on the map next to the words "Cape Fear."

* * *

So it's when. Fran is moving at 14 knots, then 16, then wobbling slowly into a kind of hover. It's a monster storm, darkening the whole map of the Atlantic between Cape Fear and Bermuda, sucking up warm water and slinging it into windy horizontal rain. It's too big to miss us entirely.

It's Monday, the beginning of a long week. We fill up the bathtub, stockpile batteries and canned goods, locate flashlights and candles and matches, fill the truck with gas. Then we load all our important documents—passports, mortgage papers, insurance policies, marriage license—into a single attaché case and keep it handy. We take lots of cash out of the automatic teller.

Landfall of The Eye expected Wednesday night, late. Wednesday is good for us, because Wednesday means south. Good for us, bad for Charleston. Hugo country.

We wish it on them. Me, Kathleen, the neighbors who drift back and forth between houses just to talk out loud, just to look at the sky. We feel bad about it, but we wish it on them anyway. If we had real magic, we would make it happen to them, not to us.

But Fran wanders north, following Bertha's path, and on TV they change the when: Thursday night, after midnight. Because our Beneteau sloop *Savoir-Faire* is moored in a tidal harbor, we pay attention to the tides. Low tide will be at 9:34 pm. From then on, the tide will rise one foot every two hours until 3:29 am. By mid-afternoon all of us whose boats remain in the community harbor at the end of our street are lashing on extra fenders, strapping lines to the pilings, watching the water lap at the bulkhead separating the marsh from the harbor.

I'd take the boat out of there, drive her to safety, but where? It would take eight hours to get down the waterway and up the Cape Fear River, and I don't know the hurricane holes there. I'd be stuck on the boat, away from my wife, in the lowcountry wilderness, with a three-to-five knot current pushing dangerous debris down the river at me all night long.

Full-force Fran aims for coast says the local newspaper front-page headline.

Everybody is thinking the same thing: don't let it come ashore at high tide.

We speculate nervously about how much the tidal surge will actually be in this protected harbor, blocked from the ocean by a large, developed barrier island—Wrightsville Beach—a channel, a spoil island, the Intracoastal Waterway, and finally a hundred yards of marsh that is dry land at low tide.

Nobody knows.

Our docks are the floating kind—they can float up on their pilings another nine feet, and all will be well. All of our boats made it through Bertha without a scratch—eighty-five knot winds and a tidal surge of six feet.

There's the standard hurricane drill: strip all sails, remove all windage-making gear—horseshoe buoy, man-overboard pole, lifesling. We all help one another. Nobody has to ask. While unbending the large full-battened mains'l, I bang my new racing watch on the boom gooseneck and break it. A bad portent.

We retreat across the causeway to our homes, where the power has already gone off, as the rain becomes torrential and the wind begins to blow in great twists of energy. It has started. So we have an answer to when. An hour later, when Fran comes howling down on us out of the ocean, it's how hard. As we huddle indoors and listen to the roaring, the question becomes how long.

When, How Hard, How Long: the trigonometry of catastrophe.

The answer is 8:05 pm, almost dead low tide.

The answer is sixteen feet of surging water anyway and winds of 105 knots.

The answer is 15 hours.

* * *

Some of the clichés turn out to be true.

The rain really is torrential, as in torrents.

A hurricane does sound like a freight train. Exactly like. If you were lying between the rails and it went roaring along over your head all night long. It really does roar. Like whatever is holding the world together is coming apart, tonight, this minute, right here, and you're smack in the middle of the program.

And your mouth really does go so dry with fear you can hardly talk.

The great trees cracking and tumbling to the ground in the roaring darkness really do sound like an artillery barrage—crack! crack! whump! whump! It takes italics, exclamation points, boldface clichés to tell about it. The house shudders again and again. Our house has too many large windows, so we run next door to wait out Fran with our neighbors. We're sitting up with them in their living room drinking any liquor we can get our hands on—vodka, beer, wine, rum—and each shudder brings a sharp intake of breath, a little cry. You can't help it. You laugh and make jokes, but it feels bad and the feeling gets worse every minute. The kerosene lanterns don't help. They make Halloween light. Eerie, spooky light.

There are times when you have to dodge out into the maelstrom of wind and flying debris and back across the lawns to check the outside of your house, to clear the storm drain and prevent flooding of the lower story. It's stupid, especially in the pitch blackness, but it feels like something you have to do. The world is way out of control, but you're still responsible.

There are freaky contradictions of nature. Paradoxes of chance. A massive oak tree that has weathered three hundred years of storms is ripped apart by the wind, literally twisted out of the earth by the roots. The next lot over, a pair of forgotten work gloves left to dry on the spikes of a picket fence are still there in the morning, and so is the fence. Dry.

The wind blows strips of new caulking out from between the casement windows but leaves intact the plastic tarps you nailed over the open sides of the upstairs porch.

There are amazing feats of heroism and survival. A man on one of the beach islands sends his wife and kids to the shelter, remains behind with their dog to finish boarding up the house, then the only road off the island overwashes, and he's cut off. He grabs his dog in his arms and ropes himself to the house, and all night long he and the dog are bashed against the house by water and wind, but they make it through. The dog was a boxer.

Lightning strikes the home of an old couple and it catches fire. Two young men appear out of the storm, attack the fire with a garden hose and keep it from taking the house until the fire trucks arrive, then disappear. Nobody knows who they are or where they came from. The old couple believes they are angels.

There are tales of death. Another man is seen stepping onto his front porch as the hurricane hits. They find him in the morning miles away, floating face-down in the Intracoastal Waterway. A woman rescued from a mattress floating in the marsh dies anyway.

For a week afterward, urban rescue workers prowl the wrecked homes along the beach with dogs, sniffing out the bodies of the ones who wouldn't leave.

It's also true, the cliché about the capriciousness of nature and about blind luck. Three Marines in a Mustang are swept off the road by the rushing water. One is washed to the far shore and stumbles into a shelter. The second clings to a tree limb for nine hours until he is rescued. The third drowns.

There are things that are outrageously unfair. A family down the street gets flooded out on the ground floor. They scramble upstairs ahead of the surge. But the battery of their brand new car shorts out in the rising water, and it catches fire. The garage underneath the house burns. Soon the whole house is burning. Incredibly, at the height of the hurricane, the volunteer firemen arrive. They maneuver their pumper through waist-deep water. But they can't get the electric garage door open and have to axe it down. And by then the family is smoked out, the house is partly destroyed, the car is a hulk.

Hurricane, flood, fire, all at once.

Thunder and lightning come in ahead of the hurricane. Tornadoes spin off the leading edge like missiles, knocking out bridges, tearing holes in houses, twisting trees out of the earth and flinging them into power lines.

Biblical stuff.

Furious Fran unforgiving, the local newspaper says, again on page one, unable to let go of the corny habit of alliteration.

* * *

What they don't tell you about hurricanes is the heat.

The oppressive stillness of the stalled atmosphere the day before the winds start. The hundred degrees of swampy humidity the day after, before the torrential rains resume. The air conditioning is off, the windows are latched down tight. An hour into the storm, everything you touch is greasy. You put on a fresh shirt and sweat it through before you can fasten the buttons.

And then the bees arrive. Swarming, disoriented, stinging, bees gone haywire. Bumblebees, wasps, yellowjackets, hornets. I'm no entomologist—they all sting.

After a hurricane, the radio warns, that's when the injuries start. Bee stings are number one, followed by poisonous snakebites and chainsaw cuts.

When the rains resume a day and a half after Fran passes, the yard is jumping with frogs and toads. Little bright green treefrogs with suction cups on their feet, smaller than a penny. Black toads the size of your fist. Giant croaking bullfrogs that splash around like rocks. Rat snakes. Water moccasins. Copperheads.

What's next—locusts? Well, not exactly: crickets. By the millions. All over the debris, the backyard deck, the wrecked boats.

But the birds are gone.

* * *

The water is off.

After sweltering hours clearing the tree limbs out of the road, pulling limbs off cars and shrubs, dragging downed trees off the driveway, raking the mess off the steps and walks and deck, my wife and I shower by pouring buckets of cold water, saved in the bathtub, over our soapy heads and bodies. We are scraped and cut and bruised and stained with pine resin that does not wash off. Every pair of shoes we own is wet and muddy and will not dry. The house is tracked with mud and debris, and a lethargic depression sets in—part physical exhaustion from relentless manual labor in the heat, from two sleepless nights in a row. Part emotional exhaustion. Grief.

We were luckier than many. It just doesn't feel that way.

When the power comes back on, it's like a religious experience. Everything becomes possible again—bright lights, cool air, television news, ice.

Then after a few hours it goes off again.

* * *

What they don't tell you about hurricanes is that the Big Hit is the beginning, not the end. Fran has swept on up the coast, taking the Weather Channel and CNN with it. On the networks, things are happening in Bosnia, Chechnya, Indonesia.

Here in Hurricanelandia, it's raining eight inches in three hours on top of ten inches that came in with Fran. They predict it will rain for another week. All the low country rivers are cresting, shouldering through the wreckage of human cities toward the sea.

Our house is an island surrounded by rushing water two feet deep, and it's back out into the storm wearing Red Ball boots, clearing out clogged gutters on an aluminum ladder, counting the seconds between lightning and thunder, counting how long to dare such foolishness. Then slogging out onto the muddy access road behind the house to rake out the clogged storm culvert, trying not to get carried into the muddy water.

On the local radio, the jocks are chatting about this and that and the other, but for hours nobody gives a weather report. When will it stop raining? Will it stop raining? The phone is working. A friend from across town, where they have power, calls. Look out your window—is it raining there? The edge of the cloud is moving over us now, she says, and there's sun behind it.

The water recedes, and now it's time to clean out the flooded garage. At dusk, the generators go on. It gets dark and noisy. We will wake to the lumber-camp sound of chainsaws.

For weeks and weeks.

What they don't tell you about a hurricane is that it just seems to go on and on.

* * *

But the worst of it is not captured on the awesome helicopter videotape of destruction. The worst of it is waking up to the new stillness of the morning after, when the wind has finally quit and the rain has slacked and the sun may or may not be up yet, the sky is just a gray slate of clouds.

Overnight, the world has changed in some important, irrevocable way. You can just feel it.

My neighbor John is standing outside waiting. "You ready?" he says, and I nod.

Half a mile away, the approach to the harbor is littered with dockboxes, paddles, small boats, lifejackets. Like a shipwreck has happened to the whole neighborhood. The houses by the harbor have taken a beating. A 44-foot sportfishing boat lies on its side on a front lawn, and my stomach turns. That's how high the water rose.

A few nights earlier, I had stood on our dock talking quietly with an old friend, admiring the sleek, trim lines of Savoir-Faire under starlight, feeling lucky. Thirty-two feet of beautiful racing yacht, a dream of fifteen years of saving come true. I'd take *Savoir-Faire* out onto the broad back of the Atlantic and race her hard, rail down, or just jog along in mild breezes, clearing my head, sharing her with friends, or filling up with the good strength that comes from working a yare boat alone.

The harbor was demolished. Boats and docks were piled up like a train wreck. Boats were crushed, sunk, broken, smashed, aground. Some were simply gone.

Out in the middle of the harbor, alone, *Savoir-Faire* lay impaled on a piling, sunk by the bows, only her mast and transom rising above the dirty water.

What they don't tell you about hurricanes is how many ways they can break your heart.

Photo credit: Larry Blokely, Silver Streak

Philip Gerard

Philip Gerard, a native of Newark, Delaware, holds a B.A. in English and Anthropology from the University of Delaware and an M.F.A. from the University of Arizona.

A former newspaperman and freelance journalist, he has published fiction and nonfiction in numerous magazines, including *New England Review/Bread Loaf Quarterly*, *Creative Nonfiction*, *Hawaii Review*, *Hayden's Ferry Review*, and *The World & I.* He is the author of three novels: *Hatteras Light* (Scribners 1986; Blair/ Salem paper 1997), *Cape Fear Rising* (Blair 1994, paper 1997), *Desert Kill* (William Morrow 1994; Piatkus in U.K. 1994); and two books of nonfiction, *Brilliant Passage: A Schooning Memoir* (Mystic 1989) and *Creative Nonfiction—Researching and Crafting Stories of Real Life* (Story Press 1996, paper 1998), which was a selection of the Book-of-the-Month and Quality Paperback Book Clubs.

He has written nine half-hour shows for ***Globe Watch***, an international affairs program, for PBS-affiliate WUNC-TV,

Chapel Hill, N.C., and scripted two hour-long environmental documentaries, one of which, *River Run: Down the Cape Fear to the Sea*, won a Silver Reel of Merit from the International Television Association in 1994. Some of his weekly radio essays have been broadcast on National Public Radio's "All Things Considered."

He has recently completed a new book of nonfiction for Story Press (2000), *Writing a Book that Makes a Difference*, which combines his dual passions of writing and teaching; he has also recently completed a novel, *Into the Devil's Eye*, and is at work on another, *The Hurricane Republic*.

He teaches in the MFA Program of the Creative Writing Department at the University of North Carolina at Wilmington, where he lives with his wife, Kathleen Johnson, and sails their sloop *Suspense* in the Atlantic Ocean.

Surviving the Eye of the Storm

By

Mike Marsh

At 110 miles per hour, raindrops have the power to break glass. Propelled by hurricane force-winds, they become liquid bullets. On the eve of September 16, 1999, we were once again under fire.

In spite of the howling wind, I was asleep. Climbing a ladder to armor second-floor windows with sheets of plywood against wind-driven missiles has become a routine occurrence here in Hurricane Alley. My need for rest from such hard labor overpowered my normal response to noise the night Hurricane Floyd arrived.

Wilmington, North Carolina has become Ground Zero for hurricanes. It is located at the "heel" of the Tar Heel State, kicking out into the Atlantic Ocean to snag these awesome storms that brush by more southerly destinations parallel to the coastline.

My wife, Carol, son, Justin, and I live in The Tides community. Facing the Atlantic, we are protected from the surf by tiny Masonboro Island. We can hear the roar of the surf when the wind picks up and see waves washing over the dunes to chase sea birds aloft from their rookeries.

Our biggest concern during a hurricane is our marina. Seventy homeowners keep boats moored in a basin adjacent to the Intracoastal Waterway. We had frantically removed boats from the marina as sea gulls overhead fled the cloud bands that heralded the approaching storm. Just ten families stayed to ride out Floyd's fury.

In the last four years, we have been struck by five hurricanes. Houses, utilities, docks, boats and automobiles have been damaged. Lost work hours due to preparation, cleanup and days without electricity are uncountable. The emotional toll is severe when watching a hurricane approach on radar images. Having lived in Wilmington for 21 years, I am used to hurricanes. But preparations for Floyd followed the landfall of Dennis by only two weeks.

I was already worn out from cleaning up when we had to board up again.

Floyd was hyped on the Weather Channel as Storm of the Century. In spite of the apprehension of watching him target us for a week, I was asleep when he made landfall. A thud and moan awakened me. Carol had leapt from bed and tried to hide inside the closet, but had hit her head on the doorjamb in the dark. Power grids had been short-circuited by lightning.

"Are you all right?" I asked.

"Didn't you hear that falling tree?" she replied. "I thought that one was going to hit us for sure!"

Carol doesn't sleep through hurricanes. Her preparations of doing laundry and buying cases of canned food are less physically demanding than securing boats and boarding windows.

After having eight trees tossed onto our house by five hurricanes in the last four years, Carol fears things that go bump in the night. The trees that hit our house were huge. They included a mockernut hickory, six laurel oaks and a willow oak. After she woke me, I didn't go back to sleep. We watched the storm's progress on a battery-operated television until the wind subsided at dawn. Together, we went out to assess the damage.

We were lucky. The tree missed our house. Justin counted 102 years of growth rings on the shattered loblolly pine. A pine is normally harvested for saw logs at age 35. This old-timer had weathered a dozen hurricanes, including the infamous Hazel. It sprouted before the first automobile arrived in town. But Floyd snapped the pine like a kitchen match.

A squirrel scolded from atop a wooden fence that was bisected by the pine. His home had been a leaf nest in the branches. Our home was intact.

His was destroyed.

It's poetic that weather forecasters give names to hurricanes, because each has its own personality. The last five to make landfall at my front door were named Bertha, Fran, Bonnie, Dennis and Floyd. They come with extraordinary amounts of wind and rain. But how much and how long they visit has a great deal of impact on the amount of misery these storms create.

Dennis had arrived on Labor Day weekend, which is also known as "Opening Day" to my family. We had pulled on raingear and braved 50-mile-per-hour winds to participate in the season's first dove hunt.

Anyone who has hunted these rocket-propelled birds can imagine that the shells-fired-per-bird-bagged ratio made ammunition manufacturers' stock prices soar. The doves flew incredibly well, feeding ravenously in the grain stubble to store energy to migrate away from the storm.

Dennis hit, deluged, moved offshore, shifted into reverse and drowned the Coastal Plain. But his wind-speed wasn't so bad.

The rivers were full to bridge bottoms when his bully of a brother menaced everyone along the Atlantic Seaboard. Floyd was awesome, nearly a maximum designation of category five on the Saffir-Simpson scale. This scale was formulated to allow disaster teams to make evacuation and relief plans based on the velocity of a hurricane's winds. A category five hurricane is the worst of the worst, having winds of at least 155 miles per hour. In non-scientific terms, winds of that velocity will huff and puff and blow your house down. New houses here are built to withstand 115 mile-per-hour winds.

The storm was large enough to cover four run-of-the-mill states. That is why we elected to stay inside the bull's-eye. Cautious, but experienced, I asked some neighbors hurriedly packing their cars so they could leave the immediate coast, "Where are you going to hide?"

In fact, it had been nearly impossible to run. Television showed traffic snarls that left in doubt our ability to get out of town before the storm hit. We decided to take our chances at home.

Fortunately, by the time the storm hit, Floyd had diminished above ocean waters cooled by Dennis. What powers the engine of a hurricane is warm water underneath it. This gave us reason for optimism as we went to bed. Floyd's central "eye" arrived at our house on Sept. 16, 1999 at 2:30 a.m. with winds downgraded to category two—just bad enough to damage residential buildings and uproot trees.

After weathering a night that pounded picture frames off walls, we removed branches and leaves from boats and automobiles secured in the backyard. We chainsawed the remains of the storm-shattered pine. A check of our docks showed they were intact, but the marina parking lot was knee-deep in marsh grass and other flotsam from the 12-foot storm surge.

Wind had not been Floyd's strong point. But what he lacked in punch, he made up for in endurance. Up to 25 inches of rain were dropped onto a saturated landscape. With nowhere for the water to go, entire towns were flooded for weeks. Over 30,000 homes and 50,000 automobiles were lost.

People died. Eight hundred roads flooded. Two hundred bridges washed away. It took days for water levels to subside enough for many of my neighbors to return home.

After so many storms in such a short while, it seemed there should have been no more trees to blow down. The sad part is, more trees were lost. It didn't concern me that my shingles had blown off, that my boat's inner hull was waterlogged, that the pine crushed my fence. Money and labor could replace man-made structures. It hurt far worse that the prime specimens of all timberdom, the trees with the fullest crowns and best wildlife values-oaks, hickories, dogwoods, cypresses, longleaf pines—were the trees that caught the most wind and fell.

Attention to human needs was foremost after the storm. However, what damage occurred to our private wildlife refuge and the mobile home that serves as hunting and fishing camp was, to us, a question mark. Our hundred-acre woods were located in the worst area of Floyd's flooding.

It took weeks of water levels subsiding before I stood on the bank of Holly Shelter Creek, 40 miles inland in Pender County. I counted 167 years of rings in the trunk of a broken overcup oak. The tree had shaded our canoe landing. We sacrificed for years to buy that slice of property. When the deal went through, I hugged that tree. Its limbs were hung with fish skeletons covered by shrouds of Spanish moss. I wanted to cry. Carol did.

It is also a somber event to wildlife to lose an oak. Eighty percent of the oaks in the swamps had been lost to the previous storms. Now, half of the remaining twenty percent are gone. Squirrels have been hit hard. Without food and shelter produced by hard-mast bearing trees, their numbers have decreased by ninety percent. Squirrels won't return to their former abundance within my lifetime, a shorter span than growing an oak.

Ducks that formerly landed in our swamps to feed on acorns will have to fly to some other region. Deer were forced to high ground, although some died in floodwaters. We saw survivors feeding by the dozens in our flooded field of rotting corn. On returning to the low areas, they will find only brown, drowned vegetation this winter.

Animals like rabbits and quail were hardest hit, according to Vic French, N.C. Wildlife Resources Commission Biologist in the Floyd Zone. "The smaller the animal, the worse they suffer. They can't swim far to escape floods like larger animals," said French.

Everyone seemed to be worried about black bears, whose future was once grim, but whose numbers have now increased by one thousand percent due to help from wildlife managers. However, bears climb trees and swim well. As omnivores, they survived by eating dead animals drifting by on the current.

Since factory-style hog farms and poultry farms have recently proliferated in North Carolina, over two million drowned farm animals were serving as food for bears and polluting water. Turkey barns flooded, and lagoons holding millions of gallons of hog waste were inundated, fouling floodwaters with filth that choked out life-giving oxygen. Organic matter and flooded municipal wastewater plants contributed decomposing nutrients that burned the oxygen from the water.

While terrestrial creatures seem to roll with the punches of hurricanes, fish are hit really hard. The water line on a surviving cypress at our canoe landing was twenty feet above my head. Everywhere that floodwaters had receded, we could see the remains of bluegills, catfish, and largemouth bass. Redbreast sunfish, those living jewels of blackwater streams, had not yet recovered from the population depletion caused by previous hurricanes. It takes four years to grow a redbreast the size of my hand; there were no redbreast remains after Floyd.

Primitive fish like gar and bowfin are adapted to oxygen levels that approach absolute zero. They will last as long as there is a puddle in which to swim.

Chad Thomas, NCWRC Fisheries Biologist in the flooded area, said, "Many individual fish were lost. However, we have to remember that fish evolved to survive events like this. Some find pockets of oxygen where they can survive. It is too early to estimate the damage done by Floyd. But when suitable conditions return, the survivors will repopulate impacted waters."

French echoed the assessment in regards to terrestrial animals. "Although small animals are hardest hit, they also have the highest reproductive potential. Once the water goes back down, they will return to replenish the areas they left. Events like fires and floods are something animals evolved to live through. It is nature's way of starting over again."

Once spring arrives, the fertile ground left by the retreating floodwaters will generate lush greenery for deer and rabbits to thrive upon. Songbirds will flock to new openings where forests once stood. Insects they feed upon have already hatched out in abundant supply—especially pests, like flies and mosquitoes.

What is important to realize is that animals have been coping with "disasters" such as hurricanes as long as Mother Earth has existed. Creatures survive—even thrive—with change. They evolved to cope with water and wind, no matter the quantity and quality of each element issued to them. They shift their populations to fill a void created or vacate a territory that no longer fulfills their needs.

Only human beings draw lines on maps that designate their individual homes—their territories. When a human habitation is destroyed, we label it a disaster. When an animal loses his home, he simply moves to another territory. Animal populations adapt to any situation, because once water and air return to "normal" status, habitats renew themselves. What is labeled "natural disaster" by a human being is, to an animal, merely "natural." Our backyard squirrel simply built a new nest in a dogwood tree.

This essay was originally published in slightly altered form in *Wildlife Journal,* Steve Walburn, Editor, (770) 795-1550.

Mike Marsh

Mike Marsh is an avid outdoorsman who has hunted and fished across North Carolina. After receiving an Associate degree in Fish and Wildlife Management from Wayne Community College in Goldsboro in 1973, he worked for the N.C. Division of Environmental Management in Mooresville, where he lived on Lake Norman. His passion for the outdoors lured him to Wilmington in 1978.

Marsh's first book, *Carolina Hunting Adventures— Quest for the Limit*, was published by Atlantic Publishing in 1995 and is still in print. In the years since, he has written hundreds of articles for regional and national outdoor magazines, but is best recognized for articles in North Carolina's "hook and bullet" magazines—*North Carolina Game and Fish, North Carolina Sportsman, Carolina Adventure and Wildlife in North Carolina*. He currently serves as Southeastern Regional Editor of *Carolina Adventure*. Marsh also writes weekly outdoor news columns for the *Wilmington Star-News, Tabor*

City - Loris Tribune, and is a contributor to the *Raleigh News & Observer*.

Heroes of the Day

By

Dorothy Gallagher

Living in eastern North Carolina, you come to expect certain things: summer lasts six months of the year, winter is a series of perpetual rain showers driven by the damp sea air and peppered with glimpses of sunshine, snow-days are unusual but hurricane-days are not. Many North Carolinians are from somewhere else. By the time they recognize the Tar Heel state as "home," they have developed a dispassionate attitude about the threats of hurricanes.

That's not to say hurricanes aren't taken seriously, by natives and non-natives alike. When news reports are dominated by longitude and latitude coordinates, talk of upper-level convection systems and cloud formation, coastal residents everywhere sit up and take notice. Finding batteries and bottled water can become a challenge, hardware stores stock up on lumber and portable generators, and the weather jumps from a close second to the favorite topic of conversation. And when potential threat becomes real danger, thousands (sometimes upon thousands) of residents head inland, and congested highways are endured for the safety of a few nights stay in packed hotel rooms watching summer re-runs. It's prudent and predictable.

However, there was little predictability in the events surrounding the events of September 13-16, 1999. Hurricane Floyd, the second hurricane in as many weeks to threaten the east coast, forced the largest peacetime evacuation in history and displaced coastal residents from Florida through North Carolina. Disney World was closed for the first time in its history, and military and reserve personnel throughout the southeast were ordered to active duty. Law enforcement agencies, along with organizations such as the American Red Cross, Salvation Army, FEMA, United Way, local churches and civic groups, among many others, coordinated personnel and volunteers to assist in whatever way possible.

Military Efforts

The armed forces have a strong presence in eastern North Carolina, and never have we appreciated them more than in the aftermath of Hurricane Floyd. In the early hours of September 16, Hurricane Floyd, who had, days earlier, been a category four storm with winds of up to 155 mph, forcing millions of coastal residents from Florida and Georgia to evacuate, came ashore near Wilmington, North Carolina. The power of Floyd (a storm that was larger in size than the state of Texas) had weakened considerably, so many people in eastern North Carolina chose to wait out the storm rather than heading toward Raleigh and Wake Forest.

At first glance the next morning, damage seemed minimal. However, it quickly became apparent that Floyd had dumped a enormous amount of water on a region that, just two weeks, before had been drenched by rains from Hurricane Dennis. Flood levels were quickly surpassed, and what at first appeared to be a near miss turned into a dangerous scenario. Intervention was needed, and quickly, to save the lives of thousands trapped by rapidly rising water.

Military personnel were immediately called upon. Over a two-day period (Thursday, September 16 and Friday, September 17), the combined efforts of the U.S. Armed Forces (Air Force, Army, Coast Guard, Navy and Marine Corps) rescued 1225 people stranded by the flooding. Blackhawk, Chinook, Sea Knight and Super Stallion helicopters, designed for combat situations, were circling inundated towns, rescuing stranded families and delivering urgently needed food, water and supplies. In total, personnel piloted 110 missions. Each lasted an average of four and-a-half hours and resulted in eleven lives saved.

The National Guard played a critical role in the rescue operations as well. More than 3,460 National Guard troops, from as far away as Texas, Florida, Kentucky and Georgia, provided transportation, engineering assistance, security, and other services to 26 counties in a declared state of emergency. Forty-seven aircraft were placed into service, performing search and rescue operations and delivering food and water to shelters. The National Guard helped to rescue more than 1500 people stranded by rising waters.

The U.S. Army Corps of Engineers (USACE) was dispatched to 15 county emergency centers in flood-affected areas of North Carolina. Greenville, Washington and Kinston counties were significantly under water and isolated by flooded roads. More than 500 roads in eastern North Carolina were closed due to flooding, including parts of I-95 and I-40.

At the Brunswick Emergency Services Center in Bolivia, a National Guard unit from Kinston was shuttling emergency medical personal to answer 911 calls. By 11:00 a.m., Town Creek, a normally sedate tributary, had surged beyond its banks, creating a six-foot deep river over a half-mile stretch of U.S. 17.

Guardsman Spence Burton, ferreting emergency medical personnel, drove a 5-ton truck through the swelling waters to reach an elderly stroke victim. With the lines of the road disappearing under murky water, driving into the ditch was a very real possibility. The truck's headlights became submerged, but it pulled through just as steam started escaping from under the hood. The guardsman had to circumnavigate trees and debris to reach the patient. Once there, he helped paramedics load him into the back of the truck.

Two hours later, the water level had risen another foot to an astonishing and deadly seven feet. Staying on the road and in control of the vehicle took enormous effort. Water streamed into the cab and, at the greatest depth, the hood was completely underwater. Nearby, the top of an abandoned pickup was barely visible. His hands in a vice-grip on the wheel, the guardsman drove on, delivering the medical personnel and the patient to safety.

Ordinary Heroes

Military personnel were not the only saviors. Organizations such as the Red Cross are vital in situations such as those caused by Floyd. Experts on disaster, the Red Cross has the ability to come to a community, assess the most urgent needs and act upon those requirements immediately. As a result of Hurricane Floyd, the American Red Cross opened up 31 shelters (whose peak population was estimated at over 48,000 people), deployed 66 mobile feeding units and set a fundraising goal of $25 million for victims of Floyd.

In addition to the incredible efforts of organizations, many rescues that took place were acts of ordinary citizens helping each other out, often at great risk to their lives. Near Wallace, when his truck stalled in high water, Mitchell Piner was swept to his death as his 15-year-old stepson watched helplessly from the tree he was clinging to. Erasmo Mencias, a passerby, jumped into the water to save the boy, wrapping his body around the boy and the tree until the fire department and volunteers could get a boat across the fierce currents to pull the two to safety.

In Pender County, Rockfish Creek washed over Interstate 40, creating powerful knee-deep currents. A van trying to cross the highway was swept off the interstate and into the creek. In a matter of seconds, the van was submerged. Another motorist, Matt Wilde of Wilmington, dove into the water, trying to reach the driver of the van. The waters quickly caught hold of Wilde, pushing him into nearby trees. For over half an hour, Wilde clung to a tree as state troopers figured out how to save him. After several attempts, a rope was tied to his waist and troopers pulled him to safety. The driver of the van perished.

Princeville, an historic community founded by freed slaves, experienced the worst of the flooding from Floyd. Twenty inches of rain put the entire town underwater. Some of Princeville's elderly residents, unwillingly to leave during early evacuations, had to be freed from their attics where they became trapped as waters continued to rise. Rescuers, arriving in boats, had to axe through the roofs of their homes in order to reach them. Two weeks later, eight additional inches of rain halted recovery efforts and prevented the town's already-haggard residents from returning to assess damages to their homes and businesses.

Animal Rescues

Hurricane Floyd caused not only one of the worst human disasters in North Carolina history, but also the state's largest animal disaster. Rising waters killed over one hundred thousand hogs, nearly two and a half million chickens and half a million turkeys. Twenty-seven counties reported losses in what was North Carolina's worst agricultural disaster ever. The North Carolina Army National Guard was called in to assist in the recovery of hogs at Prestage Farms.

In addition to farm animals, pets are often left to fend for themselves. Shelters quickly fill with people and cannot accept pets due to state health and safety regulations. In anticipation of the potential effects of the hurricane, organizations such as Emergency Animal Rescue Society (EARS), the Humane Society, the International Foundation for Animal Welfare (IFAW), and the United Animal Nations (UAN) began contacting professionals and volunteers throughout the United States, days in advance, to begin preparations to lend assistance when needed.

Members of the University of California at Davis's school of Veterinary Medicine's Assistance Team were called upon on for their expertise on September 18. By the next morning, with the support of the IFAW, team members arrived in North Carolina with rescue equipment, emergency supplies and water gear.

Working primarily in and around Kinston, N.C., the team utilized Tennessee Air National Guard Blackhawk Helicopters for air reconnaissance, looking for stranded horses and cattle. At least five horses had to be air-lifted to safety. When feasible, team members on the ground guided horses through high water to safety. Boats were used to save cattle marooned on rooftops. Other team members opened up emergency animal shelters, setting up housing areas, identification and reclamation procedures and performing exams on small animals being rescued by the American Humane Association crew by boat.

At North Carolina State University, the college of Veterinary Medicine teamed up with the Humane Society of the United States to help care for homeless and stranded animals. Warehouse space was turned into an emergency shelter to house pets from rescue efforts in nearby counties. Faculty, staff, students and volunteers manned the warehouse, giving food, water, exercise and comfort to the displaced pets. Businesses along the coast, such as PETsMART, also aided efforts by contributing thousands of dollars in food and supplies.

With animal rescues, often the greatest need is for volunteers to help care for animals, sometimes for weeks or months beyond the initial disaster. In Pitt County, EARS saved over 716 animals. By October, only 229 had been claimed by their original owners.

Domestic animals were not the only ones to feel the effects of Hurricane Floyd. Squirrels, deer and other wildlife suffered as well. For weeks after the flooding, wildlife removal professionals were busy pulling alligators out of people's backyards, and residents everywhere had to watch their step as snakes found drier homes inside houses, garages and sheds. Even injured sea turtles had to be rescued.

Some people may wonder why rescuers go to such extreme lengths to save animals, when so many people are in obvious need of assistance. Jacqueline Whittemore, the coordinator of the Veterinary Medical Assistance Team, made the poignant observation, "Animal rescue is about humans. It's not about one horse, or one dog. It's so much more elemental. For example, we saved the horse of a man who had lost everything. He was one of the burly, stoic men we met who gave us bear hugs and told us how much our actions meant to them."

In the Aftermath

Human memory is short. After all, if we can't put tragedy behind us, we can't move on. However, North Carolinians will never forget the sacrifices willingly and eagerly made during the days and weeks following Hurricane Floyd. Men, women and children from all over the United States left their jobs, their homes, and their families to come to North Carolina and give aid, comfort and support. In the end, less than fifty people died as a result of Hurricane Floyd. While each death is a tragedy, had so many noble people not come to our aid, the death toll could easily have numbered in the thousands. And although an essay can never truly repay the debt owed, it can serve as small measure of thanks.

Dorothy Gallagher

Dorothy Gallagher is someone who has a great respect for the United States military. She is the product of two former Army personnel. In a previous career, she studied Forensic Anthropology and has worked with the United Nations' International Criminal Tribunal for the former Yugoslavia, spending six months living in Army encampments and under the protection of Army Rangers, while gathering evidence of war crimes. Recently, she turned her lifelong passion for books into a career with Coastal Carolina Press.

A Capitol Perspective

By

Danny McComas

Four years and five hurricanes. This one, the sixth, was aiming straight for the coast of Florida. It was a behemoth, and was a category four!

As it approached the U.S. mainland, meteorologists were reporting that Hurricane Floyd would strike somewhere along the coast of Florida or Georgia, and the devastation would be massive, exceeding even that of Hurricane Andrew.

Early on, strike probabilities projected this storm making landfall somewhere around Daytona Beach, Florida. Unfortunately for us, Floyd began to turn north, and strike projections shifted accordingly. First, Jacksonville, Florida, then Brunswick and Savannah, Georgia, then Beaufort and Charleston, South Carolina. The biggest peacetime evacuations took place in Georgia and South Carolina, as people escaped the wrath of this monster. On television all you could see was Interstate 26 in South Carolina and Interstate 16 in Georgia as giant parking lots, with traffic barely crawling, as people were trying to get away.

Throughout all of this, deep down, I had a foreboding sense that something was wrong. My "gut" was telling me that the storm would ultimately strike along our coast, in New Hanover County, delivering the *coup d'état* after the prior storms. How could this be? Statistically it seemed impossible that this could occur, since we had experienced the brunt of the prior four years' storms. I was in denial, and would soon come to the realization that this would be the worst natural disaster ever to affect our state.

On Wednesday, September 15, the rains began, and as the day progressed, the wind and rain steadily built up. After several conversations with the state emergency management office in Raleigh, it became clear that the storm was indeed coming our way. Immediate preparations had to be made. The first thing to do was to board up the office, and secure all documents and correspondence. Then it was on to our house, to board it up, stow any loose yard items, and secure anything that could become a projectile. We anticipated the worst, and wanted to do everything possible to minimize any damage.

It was mid-afternoon when we were finally done with our preparations, and as we began to leave the house, we realized that many of our friends had already left earlier that day. By that time, all roads were clogged with people leaving, and it then occurred to us that we could end up spending our time in the car as Floyd passed! We concluded that it be wise to stay in the house, and pray for the best.

Early on the morning of Thursday, September 16, Floyd struck, as the eye went over Bald Head Island at 3:05 a.m. During the eye of the hurricane, our daughter Laurie and I stepped outside to experience the calm. It was an eerie feeling, since after so much wind and rain, all of a sudden, it was dead still. It was even more eerie, when at first, way off, we could hear the dull sound of an airplane. As it got closer, we realized it was a hurricane hunter who had penetrated the eye to take measurements. We were not alone in this. We knew that elsewhere, there were people studying this storm.

We stayed up all night, expecting the gust of wind that would lift the roof off our house, or slam a tree against it. With nothing else to do but listen to the news reports, we were relieved to hear that Floyd had been downgraded to a category three. Not much worse than Hurricane Fran, which struck in 1996. But as the day progressed, the news reports filtering back were painting a bleak picture.

The flooding associated with Floyd was unprecedented in the history of North Carolina. It was of biblical proportions! Hurricane Dennis had made landfall in eastern North Carolina in August, causing widespread flooding. Just ten days later, Hurricane Floyd brought 15 inches of rain to an area already saturated by Dennis. As a result, this disaster met or exceeded the 500-year flood for many communities.

The devastating and unexpected nature of the rapidly rising floodwaters is exemplified by the number of North Carolinians who were killed. Early estimates showed that Hurricane Floyd had resulted in at least 44 fatalities. As rescue teams reached isolated rural locations and entered formerly submerged homes, cars, and buildings, this figure rose. The ground saturation also caused caskets to rise to the surface in at least three counties, necessitating collection and re-interment.

Approximately 47,000 homes were impacted by Hurricane Floyd. Entire towns throughout eastern North Carolina were flooded to the rooftops. Over 27 counties experienced severe flood damage, and approximately 30 downtown areas were completely submerged.

Rural areas also suffered catastrophic, flood-related losses. Much of the floodwater was tainted with raw sewage, pesticides, agricultural waste products, and dead farm animals. As a result, many homes were condemned, or moved away to higher ground, away from the floodplain. The flooding also caused massive damage to North Carolina's infrastructure and temporarily shut down sections of many major road systems in the eastern part of our state. Over 1,000 roads were closed as a result of Hurricane Floyd. Interstates 40 and 95 were closed, as were sections of U.S. Highways 70, 264, and 64. The greatest challenge was disposing of the debris associated with Hurricane Floyd, with costs estimated at $150 million. Three airports—those of Greenville, Wallace and Tarboro—were totally flooded, and significantly damaged.

Water and wastewater treatment plants across the eastern third of the state were also significantly impacted. Many shut down, necessitating the disbursement of bottled water to many isolated communities by helicopter. At least 23 publicly owned wastewater treatment plants were reported to have major flooding. Their electrical pumps and circuits burned out because of the rising waters. They had no other option but to discharge raw sewage into the rivers.

Agricultural losses approached $1 billion. This figure includes losses to agricultural facilities, many of which were uninsured against flood damage. Losses of livestock is estimated at 2.8 million poultry, 2,000 cattle, 250 horses, and 30,500 hogs. It was said that sharks were in abundance at the mouth of the Cape Fear River, feeding off the dead animals that had floated down. To minimize public health threats, state and federal officials ordered the incineration of the dead animals. Tobacco in the field was ruined by wind and flooding, while tobacco in curing barns was destroyed by the loss of electricity. Much of the harvested, cured and warehoused crop was flooded. These losses came at the heels of a time when farmers were experiencing severely depressed markets.

Federal disaster recovery funding triggered by President William J. Clinton's disaster declaration helped North Carolinians rebuild. However, massive discrepancies existed between available funds and the broad needs that were unmet by federal and state monies. To rebuild eastern North Carolina in a way that would substantially reduce future losses of life and property, the state sought a total of $4.3 billion from the federal government. By December 31, 1999, the federal government had committed to allocating $2.2 billion. The federal budget for 2000-2001 contained an additional $243 million in emergency aid for hurricane victims.

To meet additional needs, during late October and all through November, Governor James B. Hunt began holding meetings to determine what options were available for relief and recovery efforts, and to search for state funding availability. I was honored when, on attending the first meeting, I found that I was one of a handful of House Members participating.

A temporary sales tax was discussed, but it was rapidly discarded as an option, since those seeking relief would also be paying the tax. Also, no broad support for this measure existed throughout the state. A bond referendum was also considered, but ultimately, it was agreed that the "rainy day fund" would be tapped for nearly $282 million, another $40 million would be appropriated from the "general fund," and $504 million would be reallocated from funds appropriated for 1999-2000 and previous years for operation and maintenance of state agencies, repairs, renovations and other capital projects. I was delighted when I learned that a construction contract had already been signed for our Fort Fisher Aquarium Renovation project, and that the Aquarium would not suffer reallocation or loss of funds.

In response to Governor Hunt's proclamation of December 9, the North Carolina General Assembly convened in an extra "Special Session." By then, there was widespread support from most members for the relief and recovery plan, and in two days it was legislated!

1999 was not only significant in that it heralded the end of the old millennium, but in that it left a legacy of water for many North Carolinians. It will take many years for those who suffered to reclaim their lives, but ultimately, our devastated communities will rebuild and be stronger than ever. Eventually, we will look back on Hurricane Floyd with the same perspective we bring to memories of Hurricane Hazel. Both were storms that brought tragic yet heroic times to North Carolina, the Old North State, where the weak grow strong and the strong grow great.

Daniel F. McComas

Daniel F. McComas has served in the 13th House District-New Hanover County (Part) of the N.C. House of Representatives since 1995. His Committee Assignments include those of Environment, Public Utilities, Transportation, Economic Development, and Highway Safety. He serves on the Board of Directors of the Coastal Entrepreneurial Council, on the Committee of 100, and is an Executive Board Member of the Cape Fear Council—Boy Scouts of America. Representative McComas is the President of MCO Transport, Inc. in Wilmington, where he lives with his wife, Betty, and their two children, Francis and Laureen.

Part IV Sorry We're Closed

Photo credit: Wilmington Star-News staff photo/Ken Blevins

Floyd Blues: Shared Devastation

By

Barbara Brooks

Unlike other traumas, which mostly affect one person or one family or at most a few families, natural disasters usually traumatize whole communities. The physical disruption caused by a natural disaster may last for months or even years, and can leave people without jobs, homes, or schools. Prolonged intense anxiety takes a toll on our physical and mental well-being. Stress wears us down and makes us more susceptible to colds; it makes us irritable, causes us difficulty concentrating and often leads to our making mistakes and having poor judgment.

Why was Floyd so unsettling? Most people who experienced the storm mention the following:

* Loss of Normal Emotional State. From June 1st to November 30th, hurricane anxiety becomes manifest. In August of this year Floyd followed quickly upon Dennis, who came, went and then returned, thereby creating a prolonged state of disquiet and tension. Eastern North Carolina's residents felt their stress and worry increase as the Weather Channel and local news programs tracked Floyd from the mid-Caribbean up the United States' eastern coast, and predicted a mighty storm approaching category five. Each new identification of expected landfall (Florida, Charleston, Myrtle Beach) brought about a brief feeling of relief, which was then followed by even more intense anxiety as the expected landfall shifted and Floyd appeared to be heading toward Wilmington.

According to people who lived through the hurricane, news of Floyd's expected landfall in Wilmington brought about a separate set of fears and anxiety. I recall a story told by a woman who worried over what to take with her as she left her boarded-up house. "Certainly," she said, "I knew the Red Cross list: important papers, medicine, valuables, family photos, some clothes. But as there was still room in the car, what should I take? Ridiculously I threw in my very best suit, leather jacket and evening dress. I knew if the house blew away I would never replace them." Then while driving away, she thought, "Well, I'll be the best dressed person in the shelter."

* **Loss of One's Sense of Security.** Hurricanes are unpredictable. Even if a hurricane is expected, the intensity of the natural occurrence cannot accurately be determined ahead of time. People cannot fully prepare themselves for these events. After Floyd, there were constant physical reminders of the disaster as the community tried to recover: buildings remained boarded up, homes were made uninhabitable by floodwater, and pets were lost or abandoned. People who experienced Floyd worry about the next disaster: Will it come next week or next year? The uncertainty haunts them.

* **Loss of Familiar Surroundings.** Landmarks orient us in our community and give us the comforting feeling of being home. We feel lost when the fast-food restaurant on the corner or the big tree in front of our neighbor's house is gone. The residents of flooded counties spoke of how strange and disorienting it was to row over what had been roads. They could no longer identify the street where they lived. To the people living in those communities, it no longer looked like home because the hurricane had flooded all of the familiar signposts that were the landmarks of their daily lives.

* **Loss of Personal Possessions.** Hurricanes can result in a loss of some, most or even all of our personal possessions. Much of what is lost is irreplaceable: heirlooms, mementos, photos, those special things that gave comfort. I remember a story told by a soldier who was not at home when the storm hit. After the floodwaters had subsided, he was having difficulty getting to his house. About two blocks from his house he suddenly stopped.

There, tucked in a tree, was a stuffed toy that had been his since he was a little boy. Seeing his toy abandoned brought home to this tough soldier all the losses he had suffered in the hurricane, and he sat down on the curb and cried.

The degree to which each of us experienced Floyd without being overwhelmed depended on a number of personal characteristics and storm-related factors.

* Personal characteristics:
1. Prior experience of trauma (too much, and it could be the straw that breaks the camel's back; too little, and you likely haven't developed adequate coping skills).
2. Support network of family and friends.
3. Prior mental state—whether you are often depressed or overly anxious.

* Storm-related factors:
1. Was Floyd actually life-threatening to you, or did you believe that it was?
2. Did the death of a person or pet occur?
3. How much damage did your home sustain? Can you still live in the house, or was the destruction so great that major reconstruction is necessary to make it safe again?
4. How much money will you be getting to help you rebuild? Will the funds from insurance and the Federal Emergency Management Agency (FEMA) be enough, or will you be in serious financial trouble?
5. Did Floyd lead to a loss of income due to the disruption or loss of a job or childcare?
6. How safe do you feel now?
7. How prepared were you? People who were prepared for Floyd feel much better than those who weren't—even if their houses fell down. Those who weren't prepared often feel guilty, believing that they could have done something to help themselves and their families and they didn't.

Although most people don't develop emotional illness following a natural disaster, most show some distressed behavior temporarily. A hurricane can shatter your sense of safety, well-being and competence. Your ability to function normally may be temporarily disrupted. Individuals react with different levels of intensity. However, most people will experience some form of reaction that is outside the range of their usual way of coping. After Floyd, people reported experiencing the following:

> * **Numbness.** Withdrawal from others, feeling down, emotionally drained or "lost in a fog" and/or having difficulty concentrating.

> * **Hyper Arousal.** Feeling irritable or having flashbacks to the storm, being easily startled, feeling nervous or having nightmares.

> * **Walling off the Pain.** Others said they tried to not think about it. As one young man said, "No big deal." The normal tendency is to put feelings and emotions aside. Your instinct tells you to try to keep the incident separate from the rest of your life.

It's not uncommon to go back and forth between numbness and arousal. People reported feeling numb one day and irritable the next. To some, the experience of Floyd brought back situations from the past in which they felt helpless or out of control. With respect to walling off the pain, while it may be necessary to avoid thinking about the storm in order to keep going in the immediate crisis, the problem is that it usually doesn't work in the long run. Refusing to talk or think about what happened doesn't undo it. Often the effects break through later.

After a natural disaster strikes, what can you do to help yourself recover from the stress? Groups of Floyd survivors agreed that the following were steps toward emotional recovery, and good ways to take care of yourself:

> * **Relaxation techniques.** Stress is completely normal at a time like this. Acknowledge that you may have a lot of unpleasant feelings. Learn some stress management strategies and use them frequently. Give yourself time to recover from the crisis.

* Sleep is always important-but especially now. Restlessness, nightmares and obsessing about the event can disrupt your sleep. Make sure you allow enough time for a full night's sleep. If you have difficulty sleeping for more than a week, consult your doctor.

* Exercise can help clear the cobwebs. A brisk walk is good for the body and has a calming effect on the mind as well. Mild exercise can help combat stress, but don't overdo it. Even if you exercise regularly, over-exercising can lead to injury. You don't need that right now!

Disaster survivors also noted that there are "quick fixes" to be avoided:

* Smoking is always a health risk. Unfortunately, many ex-smokers restart during a crisis. Try to avoid using cigarettes as a crutch.
* Alcohol and other drugs. Under extreme stress people may try to "self-medicate" with alcohol, caffeine and/or other drugs, legal and illegal. When you are in pain, it's hard to tell what is enough. Perhaps the best idea is to try to avoid mood-altering substances as much as possible. They may cause far more problems than they solve. Instead of a drink, take a walk. Instead of pills, try talking to friends or to your spouse.

To summarize, people who experienced Floyd developed the following list of "do's" and "don't's":

DO
* Get ample rest.
* Maintain a good diet and exercise.
* Take time for leisure activities.
* Structure your life as much as possible, but allow that you may not be able to follow through.
* Find and talk to supportive peers and/or family members about the incident.

* Learn about post-trauma stress.
* Spend time with family and friends.
* Expect the incident to bother you.
* Try to laugh-laughter is great medicine.
* Remember something good that happened. Focus on how resilient the human spirit is, how even in the most difficult circumstances, people find the strength to rise above adversity.

DON'T
* Withdraw from significant others.
* Stay away from work.
* Reduce amount of leisure activities.
* Have unrealistic expectations for recovery.
* Look for easy answers.
* To the extent possible, make major life changes or decisions at this time. Of course, some of these are unavoidable. If your house has been destroyed, you need to make alternative living arrangements promptly.
* Be hard on yourself or others.
* Drink alcohol excessively.
* Use legal or illegal mood-altering substances.

It is important to remember that, although a person's responses—whether stress, withdrawal, forgetfulness or other—may not be normal to how he/she usually is, they are, in fact, normal responses to an abnormal situation. However, if your distress seems especially acute or persists, you should consult a professional.

Barbara Brooks

Dr. Barbara Brooks is a newcomer to Wilmington, arriving two weeks before Hurricane Dennis. She is a pioneer in treating childhood trauma, using her skills to help children in the aftermath of Hurricane Andrew, the World Trade Center bombing, and the Northridge earthquake. Dr. Brooks is a Red Cross Disaster Mental Health Volunteer and was called to the scene of TWA flight 800 and Swissair flight 1100 crashes to work with the families of the victims. Dr. Brooks is a forensic psychologist, and has served as an expert witness in a variety of cases. She has appeared on national and local news programs. Dr. Brooks is the author of numerous articles, and her book, *The Scared Child: Helping Kids Overcome Traumatic Events,* was published in 1996. She has a general psychology practice in Wilmington.

Dr. Brooks received her undergraduate degree from Brooklyn College and earned her Doctor of Philosophy degree in Clinical Psychology at the University of Massachusetts in Amherst. She completed her internship and fellowship in child psychology at The New York Hospital—Cornell Medical Center.

Footprints

By

Jerry Winsett

Footprints?

That's the first thing that came to my mind on that soggy September day. There were foot-prints in the carpet.

Hurricane Floyd had hit and dumped more rain than I had ever seen on Wilmington. Floyd: same name as that odd little man who cut Andy Taylor's hair. (Oh, Andy!!) The massive storm descended upon North Carolina and demonstrated its animosity for being named after a nebbish, rustic barber by raining on us—relentlessly.

The following morning, I did a thorough check of my home. No shingles missing. No damage, except a hole in the screen I'd torn while putting up plywood to protect the windows. We lost the top off one of the maples, but it fell in an empty area. Once things settled, I'd cut it, split it and use it to warm my house during the coming winter. We were lucky—no damage to speak of, just a lot of leaves and debris to clean up.

Knowing the homestead was secure, I got in the truck and headed for my place of employ-ment, Barnes & Noble. I've worked at the store on College Road since it opened. The big ol' building held many memories for me, and I wanted to make sure she had survived the storm.

I pulled into the parking lot and approached the front door. The power was on—a good sign!—so I put my key in the door and stepped inside. That's when I saw them...footprints, clearly visible, in the carpet. As I entered to disarm the alarm, I myself was filled with alarm as water poured over the tops of my shoes. The carpet was so sodden with water that it could not hold any more. Each step sent the brackish fluid flowing over my feet.

I turned on the lights and looked around. Mud and filth were everywhere. The tracks in the carpet had been left by one of the other managers who had arrived at the store before me and had left.

"Floyd," I mused somberly. Much later, I learned that although some water did seep through weak spots in our roof, the major damage occurred when the street drains in the parking lot had become clogged and sent thousands of gallons of water through our front doors.

As I walked throughout the store, devastation was everywhere. Many of our stanchions and displays were made of cardboard, and when the water rushed around them, they became weakened and collapsed, spilling their books onto the sodden floor. It was obvious that every inch of our sales floor had been under water.

I went to the receiving room, where boxes had been stacked and covered to prevent roof leaks from damaging them. No one expected the water to come from below. Water had wicked from each box to the one above it, destroying two to three boxes per stack—and there were a lot of stacks.

A trip to the breakroom proved that not even our back areas had been spared. Water had insinuated its way into every area, every room and every corner of the store. Each switch I flipped cast bright light on a dismal sight.

I left the back of the store and made my way over to the café. Its wooden floor was buckling and peeling. As I walked to the window, my foot kicked something: a calendar, lying on the floor. Looking down, I saw another, then another. "What are calendars doing in the café?" I wondered. Then it hit me—they had floated over from the other side of the store.

By then, my shoes were soaked through and my spirits thoroughly dampened. The phones were working, so I put in a call to our district manager to let him know what I had found, reset the alarm and left.

During the following day, the management team conferred by phone to set a game plan for reopening. Though we knew the carpet couldn't be saved, it still had to be dried. Huge dehumidifiers were set throughout the store to begin the process. We knew it was going to be a long journey to recovery.

For the three days following Floyd, Wilmington was an island. Those who had fled could not return. A week after the flood waters had risen in our store, we were finally all able to sit together at a table and come up with a plan of action.

We manifested all of our customers' special orders to our sister bookstore, B. Dalton, so that even though we were closed, those who were waiting for a specific book could still get it. Luckily, the only books that had been destroyed were those actually touching the floor or that were in displays that had collapsed.

The water had risen to a height of six inches, just an inch shy of our bottom shelves. While the shelves are metal, the endcaps and center posts that hold them up are not. They are made of pressed wood, and acted like sponges to soak up the water. Once weakened, the bottoms of the shelf units began to split and deteriorate.

Books are highly susceptible to moisture, so we began the arduous task of boxing or re-shelving our entire inventory to keep it safe. Containment units were brought in to store the boxed books and keep them from any further exposure to the humidity in the store. Even though the ceiling had been breached in only a few places, the high moisture content of the air had buckled every ceiling tile. The whole ceiling had to be removed, as did the carpet. Every shelf unit was dismantled, and those that could be salvaged were donated to charity. Two weeks after Floyd, our store was a cavern, void of its trappings and comforts—an empty shell.

The folks who worked in our store banded together and cleaned, inventoried, separated and moved books, painted and scoured day after day as we waited for our new fixtures to arrive. And waited, and waited. We answered the phone-a lot. Typically, our end of the conversation went something like this: No, we don't know for sure when we'll reopen. Thank you for your concern. We are looking forward to reopening as soon as possible.

But at that time, none of us really knew when "as soon as possible" would be.

A month later, the first truck pulled up with our new fixtures and unloaded. As the workmen put units together, we followed right behind them filling those units with books. Our "Friends and Family" re-opening gala was set, and we were excited.

Alas, not all of the fixtures we needed had arrived, and many of the fixtures we actually received did not come with the proper hardware. We had been working to get the store open for 50 days, we were four days from our grand re-opening, and the store was still without sections of shelves, info stations, café fixtures and other necessities.

But we had books. Oh, did we have books. Not only did we have all the books we had saved—we had been getting shipments to replace the books that had been destroyed. We also had the regular shipments that arrived to restock our sales...except that we hadn't been open for six weeks, so we hadn't sold anything. And we had our shipments of holiday books arriving. All in all, 1500 boxes of books arrived.

Those last four days before we reopened were a whirlwind of improvising, shelving, re-stocking and exhaustive efforts. And on the 7th of November, we rolled out the red carpet and opened our doors for a grateful community of booklovers and caffeine fanatics! We still didn't have info stations, but tables held the computer terminals where we could look up books for our devoted customers. Our comfortable chairs had not arrived, but were on the way. It felt GREAT to be open for the public again.

As I write this, things still aren't completely back to normal. We'll be tweaking things that Floyd destroyed well into the new year, but we do have books, coffee and our high standard of customer service that was never dampened by the flood waters.

And there are no footprints in the carpet.

Photo credit: Screen Actors Guild File Photo

Jerry Winsett

Jerry Winsett began his performing career singing with his own band in Clarksville and Nashville, Tennessee. He found his way to the stage at Austin Peay State University, and went on to New York's club and theater scene. From there, it was L.A.'s stage and feature films such as *Paulie: A Parrot's Tale*, *Bastard Out of Carolina*, *Radio Days*, *The Chosen*, *Sunset Strip*, *One Crazy Summer* and *Ragtime*. No stranger to television, Jerry has starred in TV commercials and co-starred on television shows including *Newhart*, *It's Gary Shandling's Show*, *Mr. Belvedere*, *Coach*, *Life Goes On* and *Live Shot*, and was a hit as the corrupt Mayor Lloyd Lloyd, a series regular, in the Nickelodeon TV series *The Snooker Report*. Jerry has written for a variety of mediums, including stage, television, films, and magazines, and is now working on a new musical called *Hell On Angel Street* to be produced in Wilmington in 2000. He is a member of Screen Actors Guild, Actors Equity and the American Federation of Television and Radio Artists.

Jerry relocated to Wilmington five years ago, where he lives with an untrained dog, a rabbit, a ferret, five frogs, a hamster, countless lizards and his wife, Diane, and son, Logan. He has recently performed at Thalian Hall in *1776*, *Big River*, *Noah*, and *The Hunchback of Notre Dame*. He is a department manager at Barnes & Noble Booksellers, as well as producing, directing and starring in productions for *Murder Mystery Theatre*.

A Different Point of View

By

James Leutze

Here at the University of North Carolina at Wilmington we view hurricanes differently than do most organizations. For us hurricanes are, in part, a way for us to repay the people of North Carolina for the support they have given us, and an occasion to showcase and hone our skills.

Universities, particularly university systems, are collections of significant and varied forms of expertise as well as banks of enormous energy and manpower. Each individual university has experts in many areas. In a university system, gaps in talent at one institution can be filled with the skills of staff at others. For instance, if UNCW doesn't have an expert in using satellite photos for mapping, we can consult a knowledgeable staff member at one of the other UNC campuses.

Emergencies tend to bring these talents to light so that they can be applied to practical problems. Take the example of one of our faculty members who had trouble returning to campus during the Floyd flooding. When he did get back, he began talking to colleagues in the computer science department about creating more accurate and timely maps using information from the United States Geological Survey. This data would then be linked to sensors in floodplains. These precise maps could be produced and posted on the Internet in a matter of hours, and they could easily be reproduced in hard-copy format.

Though increasing the accuracy of mapping technology is extremely important, it is not the only means by which UNCW can contribute to recovery from and prevention of natural disasters. Our university has already identified knowledge in the fields of environmental studies, nursing, and psychology that can be put to use in natural disasters. In addition, we have a strong community service component: Our students already participate in volunteer activities ranging from Habitat for Humanity to tutoring, and can be encouraged to contribute their time to address regional problems. The members of UNCW's faculty and staff also engage in numerous volunteer community efforts. On a day-to-day basis and most particularly when natural disasters occur, the university is a significant reservoir of talent and energy.

We are currently seeking ways to make UNCW more focused and contributory in addressing the environmental and growth planning issues confronting southeastern North Carolina. This area of the state, much like other coastal regions, faces an increasingly complex and threatening situation over the coming years. The recent hurricanes have only exacerbated a series of problems that have evolved over the last decade. A combination of rapid growth and inadequate planning—or perhaps insufficient political will to implement good planning—has created potentially disastrous situations: inadequate drainage, insufficient housing codes, houses built on exposed beaches and in floodplains, overextended and insecure sewer systems, and so on. No administrator or politician has willed-or wanted—these things to happen, but like Topsy, we have just "grow'd."

These hurricanes are a wake-up call: a call for concerted, community action. In this action plan, this university and the UNC system can and should play important roles. Citizens must do a better job of helping our local public officials and the appropriate state agencies address the twin issues of growth and environmental sensitivity. We at UNCW are convinced that these can coexist—sustainable growth and a healthy environment as its indispensable partner.

At the university, we can provide economic data and scientific research to help guide local officials in planning. We can hold conferences and symposia on particular problems from hurricanes to water quality issues. We can help foster an atmosphere of regional cooperation, a vital part of wise planning, by bringing regional officials together on neutral ground. What better place to foster regionalism than a regional university?

The staff of UNCW has an incredible opportunity to give back to their community and practice their expertise on an ongoing basis, rather than waiting for an emergency to do so. If we take advantage of this situation, not only will we be more appreciated in our region—we will also become a better, more vibrant university.

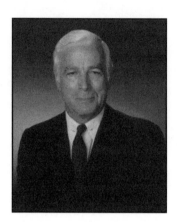

James Leutze

Dr. James R. Leutze assumed the chancellorship of the University of North Carolina at Wilmington in July, 1990. He is the fifth chief administrator of the institution since its founding in 1947. Dr. Leutze is now one of the longest serving chancellors in the UNC system and is one of only two who has also served in the teaching ranks for the State of North Carolina. Between teaching and administration, he has devoted 28 years to higher education in the North Carolina system.

In an effort to bring subjects of international interest to N. C. Public TV, Dr. Leutze worked to create **Globe Watch**, an international series that aired for 14 years. After coming to UNCW he used the television medium to bring attention to environmental and water quality issues. The first program, *River Run: Down the Cape Fear to the Sea*, won national awards, but more importantly brought legislative attention to the plight of North Carolina's rivers. The third program, *Currents of Hope: Reclaiming the Neuse River*, aired in the spring of 1999, and there are signs that it may encourage more cooperation in cleaning up the Neuse River. All of his programs have sought to extend the educational reach of the University of North Carolina. Consequently all programs come with study guides for public school teachers and are furnished free to libraries across the state.

Hurricane Floyd's Impact on North Carolina Businesses

By

Kenneth Wilson, John R. Maiolo, John C. Whitehead, Marieke Van Willigen, Bob Edwards

Until 1996, for many North Carolinians, Hurricane Hazel and the other hurricanes of the 1950s provided the benchmark for measuring our natural disasters. We used our experiences with these storms to gauge the severity of the adverse impacts to life and property inflicted upon the state by repetitive weather events. Several occurrences have collectively transformed that perception. First, there were the tandem catastrophes of Hurricanes Bertha and Fran in 1996 and then the impact of Bonnie in 1998. The second occurrence stemmed from the demographical and developmental changes that have taken place in eastern North Carolina since Hazel struck in 1954. In the aftermath of Bertha and Fran, the state recognized its heightened vulnerability to damage inflicted by a steady barrage of weather events—hurricanes, tornadoes, heavy rains.

Even less severe weather events—e.g., the flow of Northeasters and Southwesters, which consistently batter our coastal counties, and especially our barrier islands—have been reconceptualized in the eyes of many citizens and policymakers as common and increasingly hazardous. In other words, we recognize that it no longer takes a Hazel, Bertha, Fran, or Bonnie to inflict extensive damage, injury, and loss of life. Other recurring weather events—including some that have, historically, been viewed as mild or benign, such as ten-year rainfalls, gale force winds, down shears, and small tornadoes—now pose serious threats to public safety and property, and need to be prepared for accordingly.

On August 25, 1998, Hurricane Bonnie—a category three—slammed into coastal North Carolina, causing 1.5 billion dollars in evacuation and impact costs, according to a study conducted by the Departments of Sociology, Economics and Regional Development Services at East Carolina University. A great deal of activity followed, most notably involving the North Carolina Division of Emergency Management. This agency initiated the development of models for evacuation and the mitigation of damage in the wake of Hurricanes Bertha and Fran. In the aftermath of Bonnie, these efforts were greatly intensified.

It had become fairly clear that, due to the explosive development and increasing population density in the coastal zone east of I-95, such natural disasters were causing substantially more damage than they had in the past. Eastern North Carolina's heightened vulnerability to weather events results, in large part, from the gradual transformation that region experienced from the 1950s to the 1990s. The area grew from a collection of sparsely populated rural and coastal communities comprised predominantly of lower-income citizens to an increasingly urbanized zone of higher population density, increased property values, and concentrated coastal development.

Eastern North Carolina now supports a combination of industries, including corporate agriculture and fishing, retirement, recreation, higher education, ecotourism, manufacturing, and soon, a major repository for the transshipment of goods and people through the Global TransPark. As a beautiful and comfortable place to live, work, and play, the region attracts people from all over the nation—indeed, from all over the world! With such explosive growth has come increased damage potential since, as Professor Riggs of East Carolina University has noted, development has dangerously and appreciably altered the coastal floodplain drainage system.

Since the 1970s, while the state's population as a whole has grown by fifty percent, coastal counties have experienced permanent population growth rates of up to three hundred percent! New businesses have started and expanded to meet the needs of this growing population. When a hurricane strikes the coast, people (both permanent residents and vacationers) have their lives disrupted. The activities of businesses that employ residents and serve vacationers' needs are also disrupted. From 1985-1995, the number of businesses in the eight coastal counties has increased by over one hundred forty percent, and the number of businesses in the 14 counties most severely impacted by Hurricane Floyd has increased by almost one hundred twenty-five percent.

A group of faculty members at East Carolina University has taken on a mission to understand how hurricanes and floods affect people and businesses in eastern North Carolina. Following Hurricane Bonnie in 1998 and Hurricanes Floyd and Dennis in 1999, we worked with the North Carolina Division of Emergency Management, Economic Development Administration (EDA) and the Federal Emergency Management Agency (FEMA) to document these impacts. Based on this research, we have come to a number of important conclusions about the effects of hurricanes and floods on businesses in the coastal plains. In this article, we will focus on Floyd, in combination with Dennis and Irene.

How Bad Was Floyd?

While most storms severely impact a small geographic area, the hurricanes and rains during the summer of 1999 impacted a large one. FEMA and EDA identified 44 North Carolina counties that were affected by Hurricane Floyd and the ensuing floods. These 44 counties encompass all of eastern North Carolina from Raleigh to the coast. The 14 severely impacted counties included Beaufort, Brunswick, Columbus, Duplin, Edgecombe, Greene, Jones, Lenoir, Nash, New Hanover, Pender, Pitt, Wayne and Wilson. The 16 counties with a moderate level of damage were Bertie, Bladen, Carteret, Craven, Cumberland, Halifax, Hertford, Hyde, Johnston, Martin, Northampton, Onslow, Pamlico, Pasquotank, Robeson and Sampson. The 14 counties with minor overall damage were Camden, Chowan, Currituck, Dare, Franklin, Gates, Harnett, Perquimans, Scotland, Tyrrell, Vance, Wake, Warren and Washington. There were over 96,000 businesses in these 44 counties. There were 34,349 businesses in counties with minor damage, 29,939 businesses in counties with moderate damage and 32,214 businesses in counties with severe damage.

Storms can cause many types of damages to businesses. Everyone has seen the roofs of submerged businesses on the evening news. This type of damage can be very devastating and can destroy the business along with the building. During Floyd, almost a quarter of the businesses in eastern North Carolina suffered some physical damage. This means that between 24,000 and 25,000 businesses suffered some physical damage during the 1999 hurricanes. These firms reported an average physical damage repair cost of almost $40,000. The total cost of the physical damage suffered by businesses amounted to roughly one billion dollars.

Business losses were not limited to the physical damage caused by the wind and rain. Over half (55%) of the businesses reported they had suffered losses due to a disruption of business activity. More than 50,000 businesses suffered an average loss of $78,638 due to the disruption. Total business losses added up to about four billion dollars. Many businesses that initially appeared to have escaped the storms unharmed had actually suffered serious blows.

For example, the storms and flooding shut down many services that businesses required in order to operate. Water, sewer and electrical systems failed. Because of these failures, entire counties were under curfew and their businesses were ordered to shut down. Across the 44 counties, about three-quarters of the businesses that suffered disruptions had to shut down because of the storms and floods. Businesses located in severely affected counties had to close their doors for as many as eight days, and those located in counties that suffered minor damages were closed for up to five days. Almost all of the businesses are planning to reopen and to remain in the same locale.

While the electrical and water system failures were fixed fairly quickly, the road closures lasted much longer. They cut off normal pick-up and delivery routes, and made it impossible for workers to get to their jobs, as well as for clients to access the businesses they patronized. Thus, even businesses that did not directly experience flooding had a hard time making a profit. Here we see the consequences of a highway system that was not designed to accommodate business and residential development that has substantially altered the landscape. Roads that had never flooded were under several feet of water, and some remained underwater for weeks.

Once the electrical power was back on and the roads were reopened, businesses still had to deal with the continuing implications for their employees. While injuries were rare, employers had to deal with over 30,000 employees who were temporarily or permanently displaced. Because the storm impacted housing in such a large geographic area, even renters had a hard time finding new housing. Many people moved in with friends or relatives while they continued to search for a new home. Property owners discovered that it could take up to two years of repairs to render their houses inhabitable. Such stress and uncertainty inevitably affected job performance. Businesses in eastern North Carolina will be dealing with employee problems related to the 1999 hurricanes for several years.

Most businesses carried some insurance, but almost one out of every six small companies reported having none. While most had liability, property, casualty and fire insurance, they were not insured for loss of revenue or floods. Fewer than half reported that their insurance would cover replacement costs. When business owners were asked to estimate the proportion of their losses covered by insurance, their average estimate was 17.6 percent. Large businesses had better coverage than small businesses (twenty-nine percent vs. fifteen percent).

How did businesses respond to all this disruption and lost revenue? Almost ten percent of the businesses that had experienced some storm damage reduced their labor force. Over half of the firms that reported a reduction in their labor force reduced their employment by one or two employees. Less than 0.2 percent reported a reduction of 100 employees or more. The average loss was only 0.52 employees per business. Projected over the entire region, an average loss of 0.52 employees per affected business points to an overall reduction in the labor force of about 31,000 jobs (mostly from reductions of one or two employees).

In addition to cutting their operating expenses, businesses trimmed their expansion plans. Before the storms, almost fifteen percent of the small businesses and seventeen percent of the medium-sized businesses had plans to expand. This statistic dropped to twelve percent of the small businesses and five percent of the medium-sized businesses after the hurricanes hit. Prior to the 1999 hurricane season, almost one-fourth of the large businesses in eastern North Carolina planned to expand; this number dropped to seven percent.

Perhaps our most important discovery is that the cumulative effect of all the small disruptions to eastern North Carolina's businesses had as severe an impact on the region's economy as did the massive flooding and destruction suffered by businesses located in or near the 500-year floodplain. For a region where employment is hard to come by in the best of times, the loss of 31,000 jobs is significant. So is the potential loss of planned expansion. In spite of this, almost two-thirds of these businesses generously participated in community relief and recovery, giving an average of $5,800 to recovery efforts. Research currently underway will explore this issue in greater detail—not only for businesses, but also for households, voluntary associations (including churches), and the student population at East Carolina University, a school that experienced severe damage from storm-induced flooding.

Order in photo from left: Marieke VanWillingen, Bob Edwards, John C. Whitehead, Ken Wilson, John Maiolo

Photo credit: Tony Rumple

Kenneth Wilson, John R. Maiolo, John C. Whitehead, Marieke Van Willigen, Bob Edwards

Dr. Kenneth Wilson is Director of the ECU Survey Research Lab and Associate Professor of Sociology; Dr. John Maiolo is Professor of Sociology; Drs. Bob Edwards and Marieke Van Willigen are Assistant Professors of Sociology; Dr. John Whitehead is Associate Professor of Economics. All have experience in social policy development, with Wilson, Whitehead, Edwards and Maiolo having conducted research and published in the area of environmental and resource management. Van Willigen is a specialist in health and medical sociology. The group came together following the tandem hurricanes of Bertha and Fran in 1996; conducted a widely acclaimed study of household and business evacuation patterns associated with Hurricane Bonnie; and is now actively involved in a wide range of studies of Hurricanes Dennis and Floyd and their flooding aftermath, one of which is reported in the accompanying article.

Winds of Change

By

Patricia Piland

A voice for the ignored, mistreated, or powerless reverberates with intense strength and force, driven by passion and outrage. Honor, truth and love create and deliver the words to one's lips with ease. To try to write words with the same message, the same power to move, is a daunting task. But move and change we must. If we do not alter our course, mile by mile, acre by acre, parcel by parcel, healthy rivers, open lands, fresh air, clean waters and rural communities will pass into extinction.

Long before the floods of Floyd or Fran or Bertha, battles were fought to protect the natural order. One by one those battles, big and small, continue to be lost to the powerful economic illusions of big industry, mammoth structures, winding interstates, rapid sprawl and fast monetary gains. Naturalists, scientists, environmentalists and people still close to the land all know why, for hundreds of years, certain areas were avoided and left open, used only for the natural bounty and protection they provided. Even some economists speak for slow, long-term benefits of wise investments. However, it would seem that most local, state and federal leaders, businesses and many citizens have opted for the fast, easy route of quick, one-plan-fits-all growth and gratification. The continuous benefits of intelligent, area-unique planning and growth seem beyond their comprehension.

In our current system, environmental regulatory agencies are only empowered and directed to write permits. They are development-driven, nurturing open, constant access with big industry, but limited "find out as you can," "one public hearing only" citizen access. Even if regional personnel closest to a situation advise precaution or modifications in a permit, they are overridden by headquarters in state capitals where top positions are held by political appointees.

Since June 1998, I have become quite familiar with our current state and federal "environmental maze." On a hot summer afternoon, after avoiding and deceiving a small rural community for months, Hertford County officials, Governor Jim Hunt, Senator Marc Basnight, Commerce Department heads and a cast of legislators and Nucor Steel officials all announced the plan to build a large steel recycling facility on the banks of the Chowan River. The chosen site is located in a rural community called Petty Shore or Wiccacon. The zoning of this area in June 1998 was rural, agricultural, residential, recreational and camping. The only heavy industrial site on what is called the River Road is a site abandoned in 1985 due to contamination of the Chowan River and the groundwater from saturated soils and leaking industrial ponds and waste areas. The steel company is building within two miles of this brown field with stormwater ponds designed to overflow into the Chowan River. The construction site has the same soil types and regional high water table as the contaminated site. State agencies and even Governor Hunt now admit that locating hog lagoons on waterways is a mistake, but have not yet realized that locating industrial ponds on waterways is an error as well—despite the fact that the only difference between the two is the presence of nutrient-laden hog waste in the lagoons versus heavy metal-laden steel waste in the ponds.

About 200 people live within fifty feet to two miles of the new industrial site. Most of them live on land that has been in their families for over 100 years. Several generations work and play on quiet country roads bearing their family names. These people know the history of this area, going back to the Native American Village existing at Petty Shore when John White came up the Chowan River looking for the Lost Colony. They know the limitations of the land and the problems the Chowan River has had for more than thirty years. Realizing that their opinions and concerns were being brushed off by state and local officials as unprogressive, unsubstantiated, dumb, silly and even selfish, the community organized and took the name Wiccacon Concerned Citizens. They researched, wrote, attended meeting after meeting and talked to state, local and federal agencies. All to no avail.

This community has one major problem. They have chosen a modest existence where their riches lie not in money, power or politics, but in family, culture and lifestyle. To Raleigh and Nucor they are unimportant, of no political, financial or legal threat. They are considered too uneducated to see through the state and industrial propaganda used to assure them that heavy industry is of no threat to their own health or culture, or that of their children. Company officials promised large natural buffers, only minimal land usage, trestles over wetlands and streams, and the best environmental technology. However, once local officials rezoned 1,700 acres of forest and farmland to heavy industry, and state permits and politics fell into place, the protections and promises became economically unfeasible. The steel company cleared and started building before permits were even written. State officials who had promised to act as responsible environmental overseers and not to repeat the last industry's history quickly wrote off an Environmental Impact Statement as unnecessary.

The truth is, many industries look for small, rural communities and states willing to pay them to build. Land is cheap. Political officials are not afraid of repercussions. Local officials are uneducated about the long-term costs, environmental hazards and health threats, and are easily swayed by promises of high paying jobs and a "chicken in every pot." The citizens whose homes and lives are most affected can't organize and finance the legal structures necessary to take on the state government and a major industry. Big business and government have developed a system where communities with the least wealth, education and political power are chosen for the dirtiest industries. One would hope that a more enlightened society would find this immoral.

The floods of Floyd have been used as photo opportunities for many politicians, including the governor and the president. Recently Governor Hunt was on television declaring his new environmental awakening. Why didn't he—and others—awaken after the first hog lagoon accident, or after Bertha, or Fran, or algal bloom? Maybe they did, but went back to sleep as soon as the lead media story changed. Are we truly going to see needed changes in policy? Will Governor Hunt direct the Department of Environment and Natural Resources to stop their legal battle with several nonprofit environmental groups and require an Environmental Impact Study and more stringent air and water quality technology of Nucor Steel? Will the Attorney General's Office drop the lawsuit filed against the National EPA and support action to have power companies reduce air emissions? Will Senator Marc Basnight save thousands of acres of wetlands and road dollars by dropping the plans to build yet another four-lane bridge to the moving strip of sand we call the Outer Banks, so more people can build million-dollar homes in "harm's way"? Will the Department of Transportation take monies earmarked to build more and bigger highways for Charlotte, Greensboro and The Research Triangle, and instead expand bridges and develop stormwater flow systems under highways which dam North Carolina rivers and will again turn many communities into big lakes with the next storms?

Floyd was a natural weather condition caused by currents in the ocean and atmosphere. Our insistence on ignoring natural conditions is the disaster. Now is not the time for rhetoric, but for immediate action. Now is not the time for compromise but for courage to stand firm and make hard decisions. Continued mediation and concessions will only bring us the contempt of future generations who will pay the environmental and economic price for our excessive, irresponsible waste and consumption. The storm is not over. We are but stalled in its eye waiting for the next wall of winds. Hopefully, they will be the "winds of change."

Photo credit: Olan Mills

Patricia Piland

Patricia Poplin Piland grew up in northeastern North Carolina and was taught by her father, who was a forester and sportsman, to appreciate the natural world, its bounty and how it protects us. Piland became involved with the NCCF, the Albemarle-Pamlico Estuarine Study and the Roanoke-Chowan Wildlife Club during the early eighties. She found that she enjoyed teaching and talking about environmental issues with both young people and adults. Piland returned to school and has received both an Associate's in Science and Bachelor's in Biology. Her graduate degree concentration is wetlands, estuaries and coastal processes. Piland teaches science at Currituck County Middle School, while she finishes her thesis on soil development in created wetlands. In addition, for over one year she has been organizing and assisting a small, rural community in their fight to prevent the irresponsible permitting and siting of a steel mill on the Chowan River in an environmentally sensitive area.

What Next?
Part V Life on the
Edge

A Mayor's View from "Ground Zero"

By

Joan Altman

Whenever a hurricane threatens the East Coast, my constituents, the residents of Oak Island, endure days of anticipation and speculation about the path and the intensity of the storm. The Weather Channel becomes a magnet for our attention and the topic of restaurant chatter.

And rightly so, because our beach is especially vulnerable to storm damage, and the next storm could be the "big one." Also, much of our oceanfront has eroded away and lacks the width and healthy, vegetated dunes to protect the beach strand from storm surge and flood damage.

This year, we watched with dread as Hurricane Floyd skirted Florida and the media interviewed Floridians who were thankful the storm had turned north. We knew then that our stretch of coast was the likely target for a very powerful storm.

Floyd struck Oak Island with a blow exceeded only by the one the legendary Hurricane Hazel delivered in 1954. The storm we feared came ashore, destroyed over 50 oceanfront homes, and damaged over 250 more. Damage to private property exceeds $25 million, damage to public property and infrastructure exceeds $5 million, and the total economic loss is expected to top $100 million.

Most of the damage we suffered lies along four miles of our 13 mile-long oceanfront. However, almost all of this damage could have been prevented had we had a broader beach and a protective dune system. We know this because the other areas of our oceanfront with wide beaches and healthy dunes experienced minimal, and in many cases no, storm damage.

As we assessed the damage and started to pick up the pieces of our oceanfront, we came to understand that Floyd exposed a fundamental weakness in the way we view our beaches. This misperception applies to us in the community, our state and even our nation. If any good can result from the devastation Floyd has brought, it may be that this storm provides the catalyst for a long-overdue recognition of the value of our beaches and the need to preserve the public treasure they represent.

Our town developed like most beach towns in North Carolina. For much of the twentieth century, the clusters of towns on Oak Island were summer vacation spots sprinkled with small cottages and summer businesses. There were no paved roads and people who came to the beach had few services or conveniences. The beach was a fishing and vacation spot that contributed little economically to a very rural Brunswick County.

Oak Island has evolved into a thriving town that is home to over 7000 permanent residents and hosts as many as 40,000 visitors on a busy summer day. The beach shacks of the past have given way to larger, stronger homes with all the conveniences dictated by changes in building codes and people's expectations.

Beach towns in Brunswick County now comprise 47% of the county's tax base and are major contributors to the county economy. Tourism grew to become a major economic engine, and residential growth fueled beach property values to become the predominant component of the county tax base.

The beaches that spur this growth and bring economic opportunity and prosperity to Eastern North Carolina suffer from a kind of benign neglect, because people tend to view the beach as a "natural" phenomenon that will take care of itself. The reality is that our beaches are deteriorating and washing away beneath the prosperity they fostered. And all of us are allowing it to happen.

For example, we have recognized the need to create and maintain navigation projects in inlets and rivers, but we have not always recognized the need to maintain the beaches adjacent to, and affected by, these projects. We have recognized that many of our beach areas lose more sand each year than they gain, but we have not adopted policies and allocated funds to offset this loss.

The net result of benign neglect is that our valuable beaches are vulnerable to storm damage and we are in danger of losing the public beaches that we cherish.

It is also unfortunate that some residents of Oak Island, like those in many other coastal communities in North Carolina, suffer from a form of schizophrenia when it comes to beach preservation. That is, many residents object to paying for beach preservation with public funds. They believe they do not directly benefit from a healthy, economically and environmentally productive beach, even though they choose to live in a beach community.

Many of these people, along with their counterparts upstate and elsewhere, believe the burden of maintaining the beach should be borne by those who own oceanfront property. This is true, their reasoning continues, because the oceanfront property owners are the ones who benefit from the beach.

Our beaches have become playgrounds to be enjoyed and then ignored when the beach trip is over. Once a non-oceanfront resident returns to his or her home, the beach becomes somebody else's problem, but when it is time to think of a beach trip again, the non-oceanfront resident expects the beach to be there, to be attractive, to be suitable for recreation, and to be environmentally healthy.

The dry sand beach on North Carolina's 320 miles of ocean shore is held in the public trust and can be likened to one large park or publicly-owned natural area. It is open 365 days of the year, 24 hours a day and available to anyone who chooses to visit. About one-third of this beach is state or federal land that will remain undeveloped.

Developed beach communities along the remaining two-thirds of the coast provide the trash pick-up, lifeguards, restrooms and other amenities that allow affordable, pleasant beach visits. Most beach communities have numerous public access sites, many with parking, that provide beach access to all comers, regardless of where they live or what their income is.

The responsibility for maintaining this treasure cannot be left only to those who own beach property or those who live in towns adjacent to the beach. The public "owns" the beach and it is appropriate for the public, through state and federal taxes, to contribute to preservation of the beach.

"The beach" is the number one vacation destination nationwide, and the beaches of North Carolina host millions of visitors each year. While many of the visitors are North Carolinians, we also have visitors from all 50 states and many foreign countries. As the general population becomes more prosperous and vacation benefits more generous, we can expect travel and tourism to become an even more important part of our state economy.

The competition for tourism dollars spent at the beach is intense and North Carolina will lose its share of this revenue if we do not maintain and preserve our beaches. This loss of revenue will be felt most acutely in the beachfront communities as businesses close and the beaches' contributions to tax bases decline.

While it is economically important to preserve the beaches, it is just as important to preserve them for what they are-unique environments that are home to vegetation and animals found nowhere else. Storms and erosion take valuable habitat that is not replaced and erosion-weakened beaches do not bounce back from hurricane damage as quickly as those wider beaches with healthy sand dune systems.

On Oak Island we have lost miles of sea turtle nesting habitat over the years. In 1999 alone, we lost over 100 sea turtle nests to Hurricanes Dennis and Floyd. The turtles return to the beach to nest each year, but there are not many suitable nesting sites. They lay their eggs in areas prone to storm overwash because that is the only beach left. A broader beach with vegetated sand dunes allows development and native beach plants and animals to coexist and flourish.

We have the technology and the ability to restore our eroded beaches. Sand can be returned to eroded beaches using a process called beach nourishment. This process is used successfully on New Hanover County beaches and is a beneficial byproduct of some navigation projects. While this technology may not be feasible or appropriate for all beaches, it is an affordable, cost effective alternative for many beach communities.

In alternate years the sand dredged to maintain the Lockwoods Folly Inlet navigation channel is pumped onto the western end of Oak Island. This sand has built into a broad beach with acres of healthy, vegetated sand dunes. It is interesting that this is the only area of our town's oceanfront that did not sustain significant damage from Hurricane Floyd. Both the structures in this area and the beach and sand dunes survived the storm with minimal or no damage.

This was the only area of our beachfront to be "back in business" as soon as the storm passed. Thus, we have seen that investing public funds in restoring eroded beaches does pay off quickly and handsomely in reduced storm losses and preservation of natural habitat.

When you add this to the human toll of a hurricane's devastation, we see beach preservation measures as a cost-effective investment that we cannot afford to delay or avoid.

After Hurricane Floyd came ashore on Oak Island, we were besieged with reporters asking questions as their crews took pictures. Their focus was the heartbreaking loss of oceanfront cottages and the impact this will have on the community. The reports they filed often contained comments and opinions from people about the folly of building structures on the beach and lamenting the fact that the public will pick up part of the cost of rebuilding our community. Some of the commentary veered into public policy and suggested that beaches should not be developed because of the potential for future storm damage.

Then Hurricane Floyd, like most hurricanes tracked inland, inflicted even greater dollar-value losses across riverine areas of eastern North Carolina. The nation's attention turned from the devastation in our beach community to the tragic and unimaginable losses from unprecedented flooding. We at the beach were left to recover, and the public was left with the misperception that the way to limit or eliminate storm damage is to limit or eliminate beach development.

Hurricane Floyd has altered the Town of Oak Island in many ways. It robbed us of a part of our history, it crippled our local economy, it threatened our spirit, and it changed how we must view our town's most precious natural asset—our beach.

But it also rang a wake-up call for us. We now know that we have the opportunity to correct some past mistakes, as well as to provide the leadership, education and information to help beach residents and beach users appreciate both the value of North Carolina's beaches and the need to maintain these precious resources.

Photo credit: The State Port Pilot

Joan Altman

Joan Altman and her husband Bruce moved to Oak Island in 1984. She is currently serving her fifth term as Mayor. Joan was elected Mayor of the Town of Long Beach in November 1991 and served in that capacity until July 1999 when the Towns of Yaupon Beach and Long Beach consolidated to form the Town of Oak Island. During Hurricane Floyd Joan served as Co-Mayor with Dot Kelly, who was Mayor of the Town of Yaupon Beach.

Mayor Altman is the Executive Director of North Carolina Shore and Beach Preservation Association and is active in a variety of community organizations.

On the beach: Costly Pumping...

By

Orrin H. Pilkey & Matthew L. Stutz

After Hurricane Floyd, cries for "beach nourishment" of our eroding shorelines have dramatically intensified. Governor Hunt, for one, has suggested that 60 miles of North Carolina beaches need to be nourished immediately. But to do so, at a probable cost of $30 to $40 million a year, would bail out a relatively small number of people who own beachfront property, most of it rental cash cows, at the expense of truly preserving beaches for future generations.

The governor's response abandons the sounder strategy of moving buildings away from the beach. Since North Carolina's coast has the highest waves of any on the East Coast, nourishment is a Band-Aid solution that will be very costly and in the long run will not work.

We have studied the national beach nourishment experience for two decades. Nourishment is a costly process. For example, $22 million (mostly state and federal tax money) has been spent on Carolina Beach since 1980, which averages out to a $16,000 subsidy per beachfront property owner each year.

The Carolina Beach project also teaches that nourishment leads to increased beachfront development, with ever more people and property in danger, and ever more demands for more sand.

The following statements represent a few of these viewpoints, for each of which we offer a rebuttal.

1. We have a serious erosion problem here. There would be no erosion problem if structures

had not been built next to the beach. No beachfront buildings, no erosion problem.

2. We've got to save the beach. The beach needs no salvation. Left to its own resources, the beach will always be there in fine shape, but perhaps in a different location. Nourishment saves buildings, not beaches.

3. Beaches are like highways; they need to be maintained. Natural beaches never disappear or require the help of humankind.

4. Beach nourishment doesn't only benefit beachfront property owners; it benefits everybody. Therefore it is reasonable that everybody pay the nourishment bill. The beachfront property owner benefits from sand pumping far more than the occasional visitor. The house is temporarily protected and the value of property increases when a beach is nourished. As noted by George Orwell in *Animal Farm*, all animals are equal, but some are more equal than others.

5. We're victims of the storm too. There is no comparison between the shorefront property damage and the flooding disaster that occurred inland in North Carolina, where thousands of people lost their primary homes. Much beachfront property is rental property owned by the wealthy for whom building loss is not a disaster.

6. Nourishment is needed to preserve our tax base. There is no permanence on a dynamic barrier island. If an ocean front hot dog stand succumbs to the encroaching surf, the American free enterprise system ensures that it will be replaced on the new front row.

7. We have no other options. There is no room to move buildings back. Then demolish them, move the buildings off the island, or let them fall in. In a time of rising sea level on the most dynamic barrier islands in North America, painful options must be accepted.

8. For the mere price of a B-1 bomber we could nourish the beaches of North Carolina for decades. Perhaps true enough. For the price of a bomber we could also solve the state's poverty problem, make teachers' salaries highly competitive or make our state park system the best in the nation, etc.

Beach nourishment isn't always bad. It has probably saved many American beaches from being "seawalled." But nourishment has been and always will be a costly and temporary response to erosion. It may be the correct solution for a very few beaches. Before North Carolinians commit to a huge expenditure of tax money, all cards should be on the table for the societal debate.

Orrin Pilkey

Orrin Pilkey is a research professor, James B. Duke Professor emeritus of Earth & Ocean Sciences, and Director of the Program for the Study of Developed Shorelines (PSDS) within the Division of Earth and Ocean Sciences in the Nicholas School of the Environment at Duke University.

Pilkey received his B.S. degree in Geology at Washington State College, his M.S. degree in Geology at the University of Montana and his PhD degree in Geology at Florida State University. From 1962 to 1965 he was an assistant research professor with the University of Georgia Marine Institute on Sapelo Island, Georgia. Since 1965 he has been at Duke University with one-year breaks with the Department of Marine Science at the University of Puerto Rico, Mayaquez and with the U.S. Geological Survey in Woods Hole, Massachusetts. His research career started with the study of shoreline/ continental shelf sedimentation, progressing to the deep sea with emphasis on abyssal plain sediments and back to the near shore with emphasis on coastal management. He has published more than 200 technical publications.

Currently PSDS research focuses on beach nourishment, the impact of seawalls on beaches, evaluation of the validity of mathematical models of beach behavior, hazard risk mapping on barrier islands and sedimentary processes on shorefaces, and global principles of barrier island evolution. His research in recent years has been funded by the Federal Emergency Management Agency, the National Geographic Society, the National Oceanic and Atmospheric Agency, the U.S. Geological Survey, the National Science Foundation, and a variety of private foundations.

In 1987 he was awarded the Francis Shepard medal for excellence in marine geology and in 1991 he was the N.C. Wildlife Federation Conservation educator of the year. In 1992 he became an honorary member of the Society for the Study of Sediments (SEPM) and was awarded the George V. Cohee Public Service Award by the American Association of Petroleum Geologists. In 1993 he was awarded jointly with William Neal) the American Geological Institute award for outstanding public communication. In the same year, he received the Jim Shea Award for Public Service from the National Association of Geology Teachers. In 1999 he received the Outstanding Public Service Award from FFMA. Previously he was president of SEPM, the Society for Sedimentary Geology, president of the North Carolina Academy of Science, a member of the council of the Geological Society of America, and editor of the Journal of Sedimentary Petrology. He is co-editor and sometimes co-author of the ongoing 22 volume, state-specific *Living with the*

Shore series published by the Duke Press, as well as two 1996 volumes: *The Corps and the Shore* (Island Press) and *Living by the Rules of the Sea* (Duke Press). He has also been featured in *New York Times Magazine, Esquire, Oceans Magazine, The American Way, Fifty Plus, Smithsonian Magazine,* and *The Chronicle of Higher Education.*

Matthew L. Stutz

Matthew L. Stutz is a Ph.D. student in earth sciences at Duke.

Who Should Pay for Floyd's Damage to Oceanfront Homes

By

Nicholas Sparks

Five hurricanes have struck the North Carolina coast since 1996, and now Hurricane Floyd has passed into history. Most people will quickly forget about the storm; for me and others in this part of the country, however, that's an impossibility.

Hurricanes are part of our history, remembered for the damage they caused. Hurricane Floyd, suffice it to say, will be remembered for a long, long time.

I own an ocean-front home on Bogue Banks, an island half a mile from the mainland.

Before Floyd, the only thing separating my home from the mighty Atlantic and all its fury was 40 yards of beach and a 20-foot sand dune. When Floyd made landfall near Wilmington some 70 miles away, Bogue Banks was wrecked by the hurricane's northeast quadrant, where the winds and rain were the most severe.

As for my home, I knew the damage could be serious. Hurricanes have washed out my stairs to the beach four times. Last year, during Hurricane Bonnie, hundreds of shingles were torn from the roof and the ceiling in my master bedroom came crashing down.

This time, it was even worse.

My house is still standing, but the damage is unbelievable. Again, hundreds of shingles are gone. So are the stairs. So is the walkway leading to the stairs.

So is the dune.

The dune, my protector for five hurricanes, did its job well but will never protect me again. Without it, the next hurricane might inflict even more damage. Until that time, though, I'll have the place repaired and enjoy every minute I spend there.

Believe it or not, I bought the home for its location.

To many people, this makes no sense. Why would I own an ocean-front home in a place where hurricanes come with frightening regularity, where everything can be lost at a moment's notice? Secondly, should it be allowed and partly subsidized by the federal government through flood insurance programs? And finally, should the government be responsible for rebuilding the beach?

To answer the first question, I own the home for the same reason that people frequent the beaches—for the beauty. From my deck, I can watch the sun slowly inch upward, beginning its magical rise from the sea every morning.

At night, as my family and I walk the beach, we catch ghost crabs. We watch porpoises leap from the water as we eat our breakfast. It's quite simply one of the most beautiful places in the world.

In the United States, one of our basic freedoms is the right to live where we choose. I choose to live on the ocean. Yes, there are hurricanes, but no place is immune to the forces of nature. There are tornadoes in the Midwest, blizzards in the Northeast, earthquakes and fires in California, endless rain in the Northwest, blistering heat in the Southwest—every place has its advantages and disadvantages.

The second question is a bit more difficult to answer, because there are so many aspects to it. To begin, most new homes built on the coast must meet stringent design codes. As long as the wind doesn't top 130 mph, my home should fare reasonably well, and any damage is covered by traditional private homeowner's insurance.

Government flood insurance comes into effect only if there's storm surge damage, and it doesn't cover decks, piers or stairs.

In addition, flood insurance is limited to $250,000 for the home. The owner of a million-dollar beach home, if the home is demolished by a storm surge, will receive only twenty-five percent of the value of the home. That's the risk that owners, including me, take.

Some of the debate over this question arises from the fact that people who live in ocean-front homes tend to be wealthy, without need of government subsidy, and this is a valid point.

However, consider the following: A category five hurricane can produce a storm surge of 20 feet, just as Hurricane Camille did in 1969. In that instance, the water would reach six miles inland and destroy homes all along the way.

That's the real reason for the subsidy. It protects large numbers of people who are not rich, whose homes are worth less than $250,000. It's also not limited to hurricanes; flooding rivers and lakes destroy more homes every year than do storm surges from hurricanes. If ocean-front development is disallowed, should we disallow development near rivers or lakes?

Another point: If you want to stop the government subsidy, insurance companies no doubt would fill the void, albeit at a higher cost. Most people who own ocean-front homes would be able to afford it, but what about the people who live three miles from the beach? Could they?

As for the question of rebuilding the beach, this is where it gets tricky. Yes, beaches wash away. As an analogy, so do roads. Throughout much of the Northeast and Midwest, roads are destroyed by winter weather, yet all taxpayers pay for repairs. In that instance, it's an economic decision, since people must use roads for commerce.

Similarly, along the coast, rebuilding the beach is an economic decision as well, one that directly affects commerce for millions of people. No beaches means no commerce. It's as simple as that.

Nicholas Sparks

Nicholas Sparks is a resident of Bogue Banks and is the author of *The Notebook*, *Message in a Bottle*, and *A Walk to Remember*.

Let Them Go with Flow

By

Orrin Pilkey

Hurricanes Dennis and Floyd have passed, but their legacy remains in the army of bulldozers busily stealing sand from North Carolina's battered beaches to protect beachfront buildings threatened by the surf.

Dennis stirred up a huge hue and cry for dollars to spend on new and more "permanent" measures that would protect these structures and the highway that serves them on the Outer Banks. Top state officials propose to elevate state Rt. 12 along its more vulnerable sections, and to hasten a beach sand replenishment project in front of Nags head and adjacent towns. But in proposing these things, Gov. Jim Hunt and Senate leader Marc Basnight are promoting an unrealistic status quo on the Outer Banks.

They want to hold everything in place and protect all development—bad or good—for all time. That tactic is impossible on these, the most dynamic barrier islands in North America.

The time has come to move buildings out of harm's way as was recently done with the Cape Hatteras lighthouse, not to dump dollars into the sea by attempting to hold the shoreline in place.

The time has come for those who live on the Banks to accept that they are not living in Raleigh, and that disruption of highways and power will forever be facts of life there.

On the basis of a national survey by my Program for the Study of Developed Shorelines at Duke University, further beach nourishment projects for Nags Head, Kill Devil and Kitty Hawk will be unstable and far too costly to sustain in the long term. While too small to make much difference in storm protection, the effort would spawn increased building densities and more high-rise construction. The end result would be an ever more inflexible beachfront with ever more people and structures in danger.

Why are we nourishing beaches when the erosion problem is caused by beachfront property owners, not the ocean? The problem would not exist if the buildings were not there, because they interfere with the way beaches respond to storms.

Why are we bailing out a few property owners who were imprudent enough to build in a dangerous location and whose folly threatens the quality of the beach we are all entitled to use?

While Rt. 12 is flooded and blocked perhaps a couple of times a year, the state Department of Transportation's goal is apparently to make a year-round road that will never be blocked or flooded. This is impossible on the dynamic Outer Banks. A more realistic management strategy, which the state has followed for decades, is to move highway sections farther away from the surf wherever flooding occurs.

Residents have simply accepted that they will occasionally be cut off for a few days. The Outer Banks are not the Piedmont. Construction practices have to be different on storm-tossed islands.

Why don't we listen to the islands? When and where sand overwash occurs, an island is simply raising its elevation to respond to a naturally occurring sea level rise. Why not follow the islands' lead and rebuild the road on top of the new sand rather than bulldozing all that sand back to the sea?

The higher road would aid a natural process, the eventual shoreward migration of Outer Banks islands in response to higher sea levels. And the road would be overwashed less frequently.

Why don't we follow the islands' lead in retreating as the sea advances? This movement is gradual but inevitable and fundamental, and it includes the entire shore face to a depth of 30 or 40 feet.

It won't be possible to stop it. So why not live with it and thus live with nature? Tell our politicians to find an environmentally gentle way to preserve our beaches and national seashores for future generations and to stop throwing money into the sea.

Floyd's Lessons: Restoring the Floodplains

By

Daniel J. Whittle and Douglas N. Rader

Environmental policymaking can be a slow and arduous process. Many policymakers are inherently loathe to impose restrictions on economic activity or the use of private property and are easily swayed by arguments that environmental protection simply costs too much. Even unambiguous scientific data and/or the most compelling arguments often are not enough to convince policymakers to limit or regulate human activities to mitigate their impacts on the environment and on neighbors downwind or downstream.

Unfortunately, all too often it takes a crisis or disaster to generate enough political support to pass meaningful environmental laws and policies. For example, state lawmakers ignored repeated calls for controls on hog farms until June 1995, when an eight-acre lagoon ruptured at Oceanview Farm, spilling more than 20 million gallons of raw hog waste into nearby waterways. That man-made disaster, along with subsequent spills, prompted legislators to pass a series of laws aimed at reversing the damage caused by 2,500 factory-sized hog farms, culminating in Governor Hunt's call last spring for a phase-out of all open-air hog lagoons statewide. Massive fish kills in the mid-1990s in the Neuse river served as a dramatic wake-up call to policymakers: immediate action was needed to reduce nutrient pollution in that basin from urban stormwater, farm runoff, and other previously unregulated sources. The lessons from these crises were clear, and fortunately policymakers responded to them promptly, if not comprehensively.

Those disasters pale in comparison to the nature and scope of human and environmental impacts from the flooding that resulted from Hurricanes Floyd and Dennis. The flooding killed more than 50 people and virtually closed down the eastern third of the state, damaging or destroying wastewater and drinking water systems, roads, homes, businesses, and farms. The flooding inundated at least 47 hog lagoons and took out four others. After the floods, more than half of the state's factory hog farms had lagoons so full that they could no longer legally comply with their waste plans and permits.

Because of the magnitude of the flooding, it will certainly take a long time to assess and respond to the lessons learned from the flooding, ensuring a steady curriculum for policymakers for years to come. Nonetheless, one of the clearest lessons illustrated by the flooding so far is that the aggregate effect of past piecemeal land use decisions in the coastal plain has resulted in a human landscape that is not sustainable. The most obvious example may also be the toughest politically: Princeville. While we are quite sympathetic with the residents of Princeville in their desire to maintain geographic links to their heritage, we strongly suspect that the proposed reinvestment in that area is doomed to failure. The existing town is located in the active floodplain of the Tar River, on land that was—frankly—not preferred for settlement for good reason. In fact, a quick glance at the soil map of Edgecombe County demonstrates that the long-term floodplain extends for miles to the east. Moreover, the dike that ruptured provides minimal protection from Tar River flooding, ending abruptly on the north along US Highway 258, and allowing floodwaters to move around it and fill it up. Our fieldwork at Princeville, as verified by Dr. Stan Riggs at East Carolina University, showed clearly that the dikes ruptured only after standing water was almost as high as they were. Finally, the high dam created during the recent construction of U.S. Highway 264 through Princeville backed up floodwaters even deeper inside the dike.

This situation cannot be remedied simply by building back the dike ($600,000) and rehabilitating the residences inside the town ($2.5 million for public housing, who knows how much for private housing). A comprehensive plan based upon high-quality modeling would be needed—if that is possible. We are concerned that no landform is available in the area to anchor a fully protective dike on the east side of the town. (It might even require a circular dike with pumping to maintain Princeville in its current location.) We also expect that retrofitting the U.S. 264 "road dam" will be extremely costly. It strikes us that town residents and officials could develop alternative solutions which would address this problem fully and in a lasting manner, while continuing to appropriately memorialize the heroic and historic early residents. One bold idea might be to relocate the town onto a nearby upland site, while restoring the natural floodplain vegetation and creating appropriate memorials to commemorate Princeville and its early residents. (A beneficial side effect would be to begin restoring the natural floodplain function of the nutrient-impaired Tar-Pamlico estuary system.) In any event, rebuilding with no further improvements simply sets the stage for a repeat of the 1999 flooding, likely to occur much sooner than "500 years."

A similar situation exists at Speed, the other diked Edgecombe County town devastated by the floods. The dike at Speed is huge and of fairly recent origin. Our field analysis suggests that the dike failure also had a strong human component. When the dike was built, the watershed was modified to redirect tributary streams. The dike—again—was not anchored to a landform of common elevation. After talking to residents and examining the residues after the floodwaters subsided (again with Dr. Riggs' assistance), it is apparent that the Speed dike accumulated water up to approximately thigh level from sheetflow off the upland to the east and from watershed delivery above grade from the east, before abruptly rupturing and flooding completely. The rupture occurred exactly where high-level flows from upstream in Deep Creek are focused by stream conformation and the earthen dam created by the crossing of Deep Creek by Cutchin Farm Road—another "road dam" in action. Remediation of this problem must be dependent on careful analyses of watershed processes, and not simply another "stop gap" approach.

In both cases, it is likely that the downstream flows encountered by the towns and their dikes were exacerbated by human modifications of the watersheds involved, although estimates of the degree would depend upon careful modeling not yet available. Flow enhancement derives from reduced vegetative cover (and associated decreases in evapotranspiration), compacted soils, increased impervious surfaces, enhanced runoff from stormwater management systems (including those on farms), and decreased retention in wetlands and other riparian storage components. In addition, channelization of inner coastal plain streams speeds up downstream delivery. Ironically, the diking and channelization of Deep Creek near Speed enhanced water delivery downstream…to the Tar River just upstream of Princeville!

One model for how an integrated watershed and floodplain remediation plan might be developed and implemented exists in the Edenton Bay Restoration Plan. We worked with federal, state and local government officials, academic scientists and landowners to develop a plan to rehabilitate the spawning and nursery function for river herring of the tributaries to Edenton Bay, Queen Anne Creek and Pembroke Creek. The plan will eliminate the most egregious pollution sources (including a noxious hog farm, an old welding plant in the floodplain, urban stormwater and others), will reforest streamside areas that had been deforested in the past, and will protect high value wetlands in the watershed. The Clean Water Management Trust Fund in November funded phase I of the project for $3.28 million. Other state and federal programs, like the Conservation Reserve Enhancement Program which pays farmers to replace marginal farm land with streamside forested buffers and wetlands, are available now to start the process of restoring the floodplains.

On the other hand, failure to act boldly and decisively may well threaten the nationally important coastal resources of which we are stewards. Perhaps the most egregious example is the Tar-Pamlico Basin, and its critical fish production capacity, seriously threatened by nutrient overenrichment. The Pamlico was the "fish kill poster child" of the late 1980s and early 1990s, the site of the major original Pfiesteria blooms and related problems—as the Neuse is today. An initial framework to reduce nutrients was put in place in 1989; that framework ignored the most important sources of nutrients, from nonpoint sources. Despite significant reductions in point-source nutrients, increased loads to the estuary from wetland losses and atmospheric ammonia from swine farms and other new sources resulted in no net improvement in the Pamlico. Ten years later, North Carolina is still struggling to begin to address farm-based nutrients in this basin, the one hit hardest by Hurricane Floyd.

Opportunity is once again born of crisis, and the overall lessons from Hurricanes Dennis and Floyd cannot be clearer. It is no longer enough to throw public money at "flooding" problems. Instead a more careful approach must be taken, where pollution sources are systematically eliminated from floodplains, and where human modifications of water delivery pathways are assessed and mitigated through return to more natural flow patterns. After all, the greatest portion of water pollution problems today are directly linked to changing the way that water moves, and thereby increasing the amount of pollution delivered by it. Restoring more natural flows and more naturally vegetated floodplains will be critical elements of water basin management plans for the new millennium.

To date, most of the policy response to last fall's flooding has been focused on getting enough financial relief to those who lost homes and businesses. A relatively small percentage of these relief funds is targeted to removing development from the floodplains. Almost an even smaller amount is earmarked for floodplain mitigation or restoration. It is time to take the long view, and begin building a floodplain management program that will not only reduce human economic and environmental exposures when large-scale events occur, but will also form a solid foundation for a more effective restoration program for the lowlands which shroud our coastal zone. Such a "Comprehensive Floodplain Restoration Act" might include measures to protect existing riparian forests, but also reforest barren streamside areas, while eliminating pollution sources located in flood-sensitive areas. Fortunately, many of the tools needed to accomplish the needed restoration already exist, given the foresight of state leaders like Senator Marc Basnight and state officials: the Clean Water Management Trust Fund, the Wetland Restoration Program, the Basinwide Management Program, the Coastal Habitat Protection Planning Program, the Conservation Reserve Enhancement Program and others.

Though Hurricane Floyd destroyed many dreams, from that catastrophe can arise the formula for a healthy coast. All we need are leaders bold enough to grasp that concept.

Dan Whittle

Dan Whittle is a Senior Attorney with Environmental Defense in North Carolina. Mr. Whittle has extensive experience in environmental and natural resources law and policy, with a special emphasis on marine fisheries management, regulation of intensive livestock operations, water quality protection, and public and private forest management. He is involved in the group's efforts to promote sensible and meaningful environmental regulation of factory feedlots, and is working to develop an ecosystem-based management system for estuarine-dependent marine fish.

Mr. Whittle received his J. D. from the University of Colorado in 1989 and his Bachelor of Arts in Economics and German from Vanderbilt University. Prior to joining Environmental Defense, Mr. Whittle served as the Senior Policy Advisor for the N.C. Department of Environment and Natural Resources and practiced environmental law in Washington, D.C.

Douglas N. Rader

Douglas Rader is a Senior Scientist with the North Carolina office of Environmental Defense. Dr. Rader has worked to protect and restore estuaries, wetlands and endangered species in North Carolina since 1988. He is currently working to develop an ecosystem-based management system for estuarine-dependent marine fish. His work led directly to the 1997 North Carolina Marine Fishery Reform Act. Dr. Rader works closely with the South Atlantic Fishery Management Council, the Mid-Atlantic Fishery Management Council, and the Atlantic States Marine Fisheries Commission on fishery management and fish habitat protection. He also serves on the Marine Reserves Advisory Panel of the South Atlantic Fishery Management Council, and the Gray's Reef National Marine Sanctuary Advisory Council.

Dr. Rader holds graduate degrees from the University of North Carolina at Chapel Hill (Ph.D., 1984) and the University of Washington (M.S., 1980). He worked previously as Director of the Albemarle-Pamlico Estuarine Study, and in the N.C. Division of Environmental Management and the N.C. Division of Coastal Management.

Disaster Prevention - What Can Be Done?

By

Jackie Savitz

Each hurricane that hits the Carolinas reminds us that we have failed to prevent a disaster. Soon after a storm, local governments and private interests resume their usual unplanned development practices instead of practicing disaster prevention. To actually prevent the next disaster, we must begin to discourage coastal development in hurricane-prone regions. The benefits are enormous: minimizing taxpayer funded disaster relief costs, and protecting the environment at the same time. This should be accomplished in a way that is fair to both homeowners and taxpayers. This essay lays out the necessary solutions.

Disaster by Design

Poor planning practices can actually contribute to the severity of a storm. Much of the damage caused by hurricanes could be prevented by employing smarter, more sustainable development practices. Instead, unsustainable practices are fostered by poorly conceived local, state, and federal policies. The significant encouragement that the United States government provides for barrier island development, for example, includes subsidized flood insurance policies, beach building funds, road construction money, bridge construction costs and additional financing for other infrastructure. Such subsidies, contained in forty federal programs, tap the taxpayer-funded Treasury, and encourage sprawl and unwise development on our coastal barrier islands.

These are not entitlements that are owed to developers and residents. Rather, they are investments that the federal government makes at will. To prevent disasters, these investments should be targeted in areas where they are sensible and denied in high-risk places.

Once developed, coastal areas require a constant influx of cash. In hurricane-prone regions, coastal communities immediately find themselves mired in an endless cycle of construction, destruction, reconstruction, and repeated destruction that requires the financial bail-outs more commonly known as disaster relief. After a hurricane hits, people rarely retreat from the ocean. Instead they use subsidized insurance payments to rebuild in exactly the same place. This often means asking the taxpayer to help out again and again after each inevitable storm.

For example, as of 1995 there were 99 properties in Nags Head that have suffered such repetitive losses and been rebuilt, costing the taxpayer $4 million so far.[1] But that's nothing—it gets worse. In Kearny, New Jersey, there are homes that have averaged nine losses each, leading to an average cumulative payout per home of $808,000![2] This is more than some of these homes are even worth. Thousands of homes across the country have received cumulative pay-outs that exceed their property value, and some have received many times that value. Is this where North Carolina is headed?

Keep in mind, it is the federal Treasury, and the federal taxpayer, that foot the bills for flood insurance payouts. People in Iowa pick up the tab for risky ventures in North Carolina. Because the Federal Emergency Management Agency (FEMA) is over $800 million in debt, they have had to borrow from the Treasury to make good on the insurance policies they have issued. This is a testament to the assertion that subsidizing coastal development is a losing proposition. No corporation would continue to operate at such a loss. To stem these losses, this country should stop providing new flood insurance policies and stop making new commitments to rebuild beaches in places that have suffered repetitive losses.

Let us not confuse these bail-outs with bona fide disaster relief. There is a big difference between helping out low-income communities which, for economic reasons, are located in floodplains devastated by major storms, and providing "Welfare for the Wealthy," which involves bailing out well-to-do Americans who can afford second homes on high-priced barrier islands and refuse to

1. See National Wildlife Federation, *Higher Ground*. July, 1998.
2. See National Wildlife Federation, *Higher Ground*. July, 1998.

relocate after their first beach home is destroyed. Rejecting the "Welfare for the Wealthy" policy does not in any way minimize the importance of helping those in need.

As for beachfront homeowners, fairness dictates that current flood policies should be recognized and damages should be covered—once. To reciprocate this fair treatment, recipients of these damage checks should relocate, or find alternative private insurance; they should not expect, or be entitled to, continued coverage by the federal taxpayer.

Who Pays?

Those who insist on building new homes on the beach should do so at their sole risk, and with their own money. Repeatedly providing federal assistance for risky ventures in these areas gives people a false sense of security making them more likely to take a risk. After all, it's not their money. If they lose, we all lose. If they survive the storm, they will be made whole by the American taxpayer. What does the taxpayer get in return?

To say that every American is free to visit and enjoy the beach is an overly simplistic economic argument. Those that do visit pay for their visit. Costs for local services such as beaches and bridges should be built into hotel fees, and property and sales taxes, for example. Such is often the case with local services elsewhere. This way, where it makes economic sense to build on barrier islands, it can happen without subsidies.

However, federal subsidies force the costs of these ill-conceived activities onto people who would not otherwise pay for them—either because they do not visit the beach, or because they are not willing to pay the real costs of repeated reconstruction of buildings, beaches, roads, and sewer systems. Internalizing such costs to the local economy ensures that those who benefit from it pay for it. It also removes the false sense of security provided by the constant stream of federal dollars. If the costs were borne by the local economy, that would drive coastal development where it is economically justified. Where it is not economical, it would not happen.

Disaster Prevention

If the government denied these subsidies in hurricane-prone areas, development in such areas would be discouraged. In 1982, under the Reagan administration, Congress unanimously passed a law that took a step in the right direction. The Coastal Barrier Resources Act (CBRA) sets up the Coastal Barrier Resources System, which now contains 1.3 million acres of land (including about 33,500 acres in North Carolina) where no federal value-added program may be provided—no federal flood insurance, no federal money for beach building, highway construction, or sewer provision. People who still choose to build in these places take their own risks both financially and personally. The program was set up to meet three goals: 1) Save taxpayer money, 2) Protect human life and minimize property loss, and 3) Protect ecologically important barrier islands.

The problem is that there is not a lot of land in the System, and developers and real estate interests are constantly trying to remove the most prime pieces so that they or their clients can benefit from taxpayer subsidies. Each time this happens, we take a step backwards from the three goals, losing key nesting ground for threatened species of birds, sea turtles and other wildlife whose habitats are increasingly being invaded, filled in, and paved over.

Given what we know now, 18 years after the passage of CBRA, we need to expand the ideas embodied in the Coastal Barrier Resources System to cover more area, save more taxpayer money, protect more human lives and property, and protect what little is left of our barrier islands. To prevent disasters, we need to take the following five steps:

1) **Federally subsidized flood insurance should not be available for new development in high-risk areas.** This would discourage all but the wealthiest home builders who could self-insure or find alternative private insurance policies.

2) **Payment of damage claims should be tied to relocation, not reconstruction.** This will encourage communities to move toward a more sustainable development pattern that prevents disasters, rather than resuming high-risk patterns that ensure future disasters.

3) **Future federal flood insurance policies should not be made available to residents that insist on rebuilding.** A one-time damage payment should be made, and the policy should be discontinued if the homeowner insists on rebuilding.

4) **No new policies should be issued for new development in high-risk areas.** Withholding federal flood insurance is one way to discourage new homes in areas that have suffered repetitive losses. People may still choose to build, but they, not the taxpayer, bear the risk.

5) **Preserve natural barrier island habitats.** Local governments and zoning boards should set aside undeveloped barrier island land as wilderness conservation areas in perpetuity. Where buy-outs occur, the federal government should do the same. This will ensure that disaster prevention is a permanent solution.

This strategy follows the example of the Cape Hatteras Lighthouse, which serves as a beacon for a sustainable development pattern further back from the ocean. Most importantly, it marks a course for disaster prevention that government agencies and private interests should embark on now, before the next inevitable hurricane hits.

Catastrophic disasters in the U.S. and the rest of the world are increasing—disasters that cause 25 or more deaths have tripled since 1940, and 7 of the 10 costliest disasters in history occurred between 1989 and 1994. And even these are not considered the "Big Ones."

Source: Dennis Mileti, *Disasters by Design*, 1999.

Beach Renourishment—Costs to Federal Taxpayers

Many taxpayer-funded projects are framed as if they were environmental benefits using terms such as beach building, dune stabilization, or even island creation. But the barrier islands don't actually need these "benefits." They have withstood many a hurricane long before we got here. As many observers have pointed out, it is clearly the buildings that are being saved, not the beaches.

* In 1997 alone, the federal taxpayer shoveled over about $180 million to pump sand.

* WRDA contained about $300 million in sand pumping and other coastal subsidies.

* Long-term maintenance on these projects will cost another $330 million over the next 50 years, and we are still paying the long-term costs of every other project that has been started in the past half-century.

* In New Jersey alone, we will spend $9 billion as we struggle to keep sand on 127 miles of the state's beaches.

Source: Coast Alliance, 1999.

Jackie Savitz

Jacqueline Savitz is the Executive Director of the Coast Alliance, an organization that leads an Alliance of over 500 groups around the country to protect our priceless coasts from pollution and development. The goals of the Coast Alliance include preventing nonpoint source pollution, cleaning up and preventing further sediment contamination, and discouraging development in sensitive coastal areas that are prone to flooding and storm damage.

Jacqueline earned her Master's degree in environmental science with emphasis in toxicology from the University of Maryland, Chesapeake Biological Laboratory. There her work focused on the effects of contaminants on aquatic life. Prior to that she earned her Bachelor's degree in marine science and biology from the University of Miami, in Florida.

Coastal North Carolina: Planning for a Sustainable Future

By

David R. Godschalk

North Carolina was an early leader in coastal management. The General Assembly passed the Coastal Area Management Act (CAMA) in 1974, after two years of bitter political debate. CAMA was the state's answer to the national call for coastal management under the federal Coastal Zone Management Act of 1972, which set up a collaborative federal/state program that included federal grants for state coastal planning.

In its first decade, the North Carolina coastal program was seen as a successful model. David Owens, then Director of the N.C. Division of Coastal Management, declared in a 1985 article: "Through the successful resolution of several critical issues, including creating a local land use planning process and managing oceanfront development, the program has built its credibility, its popular and political support, and its ability to address remaining critical management needs."[i] However, Owens noted that the program's greatest challenges in the next decade would be to address protection of coastal water quality, to deal with pressures from high-density resort development, and to protect freshwater wetlands. He warned that continued success is far from assured.

One of the pillars of CAMA is the local land use planning process. All twenty coastal counties

i. Owens, David. 1985. "Coastal Management in North Carolina: Building a Regional Consensus." *Journal of the American Planning Association,* vol. 51, no. 3, pp. 322-329.

are required to prepare comprehensive land use plans and to update these plans on a regular basis. Planning guidelines are specified in the North Carolina Administrative Procedures Act, Subchapter 7B, which states that land use planning offers the best chance for developing a common vision and goals for the future that balance the economic development and resource protection necessary for a healthy coast.

Under the guidelines, land use planners must collect and analyze data about present conditions and future demands, including land suitability for development and community services capability, and projected ten-year population growth as the basis for future land needs. Plans must contain policy statements on resource protection, economic and community development, and hazard mitigation, and include a vision of the community in the next ten years. The core of the plans is a system of land classification, which specifies developed, urban transition, community, rural, and conservation areas on a future land use map. Growth is to be directed into the urban transition areas where the land is suitable for development and supporting urban services will be provided. The Coastal Resources Commission, consisting of 15 members appointed by the governor, reviews the plans for technical accuracy and consistency. It may reject plans that are inconsistent with the state's Coastal Management Plan.

A second pillar of CAMA is the designation of Areas of Environmental Concern (AECs). Within these designated areas, all major development proposals must be approved for a permit by the Coastal Resources Commission. The AECs include such things as coastal wetlands, estuarine waters, renewable resource areas, fragile natural resource or historic areas, public trust areas, and natural hazard areas.

In theory, the AEC permitting process should be sufficient to protect critical coastal environmental areas. However, in practice, the AEC designations only cover small geographic areas, and unless backed up by strong protective management of adjacent areas, the AEC permit process alone is inadequate. This is because the natural resources designated as AECs are elements of interconnected ecological systems, and the "patches" of AEC designation do not take into account the system connections or the impacts of development next door.

There are disturbing signs that the CAMA approach to coastal management, seen as successful by Owens in 1985, is not working effectively in 1999. The purpose of this essay is to explore the present status of land use planning in the coastal area and to suggest potential changes that may solve some of its current problems and enable it to contribute to a healthy and sustainable coastal environment in the future.

CAMA Planning is Not Producing a Sustainable Coastal Region

Sustainable development is development that meets present needs without compromising the ability of future generations to achieve their needs. Sustainable development lives on the "interest" yielded by natural systems, rather than using up their "capital." It maintains the ecological integrity of the natural systems to regenerate themselves. Sustainable development balances economic development, environmental conservation, and social equity, rather than focusing only on one objective.

For coastal North Carolina, sustainable development must be measured by the ongoing conservation and health of the natural resource systems—our coastal commons. It is unsustainable to allow the ditching and draining of 10,000 acres of freshwater wetlands, as was reportedly allowed by the state in 1998 and 1999.[ii] Clearly, that is using up environmental capital. Recruiting a polluting industry, such as a steel mill, to the rural coastal area along a river with a history of environmental problems, such as the Chowan River, does not appear to strike a reasonable balance between economic development and environmental conservation.[iii]

Sustainable development demands responsible management by state agencies, as well as coastal local governments—a sustainable partnership. That was to have been the cornerstone of CAMA.

Evidence is clear for all to see that twenty-five years of coastal management under CAMA have not resulted in sustainable urban development patterns for the present generation, much less for

ii. According to the North Carolina Coastal Federation's 1999 *State of the Coast Report*, state officials estimate that up to 10,000 acres of wetlands were ditched in New Hanover, Brunswick and Pender counties in six months after the state announced it would not enforce wetland protection rules for that period due to lack of staff.

iii. The 1999 *State of the Coast Report* outlines the chronology of the recruitment of Nucor Steel with $161 million in state tax incentives and a questionable environmental assessment process to a site on the nutrient-sensitive waters of the Chowan River, across from the Chowan Swamp State Natural Area, an important fish spawning location.

iv. See North Carolina Coastal Futures Committee. 1994. *Charting a Course for Our Coast: A Report to the Governor*. Raleigh, Division of Coastal Management; and North Carolina Coastal Federation. 1999. *State of the Coast Report*. Vol. 17. No. 4.

v. A concerned group of coastal scientists delivered a statement to the governor in January 1999, stating the belief that the environmental health of North Carolina's estuarine waters, streams, rivers, and sounds has declined dramatically during the last twenty-five years. They found that CAMA has not been able to protect coastal waters from development's impact and called on elected state officials to stop the growing degradation of these waters.

future generations.[iv] Predictable, regular extreme events, such as Hurricane Floyd, Dennis, and Fran, generate avoidable flooding, pollution, and devastation of built-up areas. Shellfish areas are regularly closed due to pollution from urban runoff. It doesn't take an environmental scientist to see that we are doing something wrong.[v]

CAMA land use plans were supposed to balance economic growth and environmental protection, but somehow planners never found the right way to do this. Despite some successes in enforcing reasonable coastal construction setbacks and prohibiting coastal armoring, the Coastal Resources Commission has not found the right combination of state guidelines, technical assistance, and funding for land use planning by local governments to achieve this vital balance. Admittedly, local land use plans are just one part of the sustainable development equation—but they are a critical part.

Failures of CAMA Land Use Plans

What's wrong with the CAMA land use plans? A recent study by Professor Edward Kaiser and his colleagues at the University of North Carolina at Chapel Hill, who surveyed local governments and analyzed local North Carolina land use plans, highlights the failures of CAMA land use plans.[vi] Plan content consists of a number of components. Those analyzed in the Kaiser study include:

- Data collection and analysis: the facts and projections of population, economy, land use, water, environment, and the like, on which the plans are based.
- Goals and values specified in the plans: explicit statements of desired achievements.
- Policies on land use, regulations, intergovernmental coordination, and capital improvements: spatially-specific designs for urban and conservation areas.
- Water resources: how the plans addressed water quality issues and protection tools.
- Implementation: how the plans will be carried out by local government regulations and spending.
- Monitoring and evaluation: how the plans' performances will be tracked, and which bench

vi. Overall statewide study results and recommendations are reported in two articles: Sara Hinkley and Edward Kaiser. 1999. "Making the Land Use-Water Quality Connection." Carolina Planning, Vol. 24, no. 1, pp. 29-39; and Edward Kaiser and John Davies. 1999. "What a Good Local Development Plan Should Contain." Carolina Planning Vol. 24, no. 2, pp. 29-41. The data for this essay are from a coastal plan database of 26 plans created by Megan Owen for the author, from the larger statewide database of 98 local plans analyzed by Kaiser and his colleagues.

marks will be used for judging its effectiveness.

• Overall plan quality: consistency, clarity, and readability of the plan document and maps.

Kaiser and his colleagues read 26 CAMA plans and analyzed their content. They rated each component of the plans on a four-point scale running from 0 to 3. A rating of 0 indicates a missing or weak plan component; a rating of 1 indicates an adequate but not detailed plan component; a rating of 2 indicates a high-quality plan component; and a rating of 3 indicates an excellent or model plan component.

To put this rating scheme into commonly understood terms, I translated this four-point scale into letter grades for the plan elements. Thus, a 'zero' rating equals a grade of D-F; a 'one' rating equals a grade of C; a 'two' rating equals a grade of B; and a 'three' rating equals a grade of A. The table below shows the grades for the individual components of the 26 CAMA plans that Kaiser and his colleagues assessed.

Results of CAMA Land Use Plan Evaluation				
Plan Grades Number (percent)	**D—F** (Missing or weak)	**C** (Adequate)	**B** (Good)	**A** (Excellent)
Data analysis:	1 (4%)	14 (54%)	9 (35%)	2(8%)
Goals & values	14 (54%)	9 (35%)	2 (8%)	1 (4%)
Policies	3 (12%)	13 (50%)	9 (35%)	1 (4%)
Water resources	2 (8%)	11 (42%)	11 (42%)	2 (8%)
Implementation	19 (73%)	6 (23%)	1 (4%)	0
Monitoring/evaluation	23 (88%)	3 (12%)	0	0
Overall plan quality	4 (15%)	12 (46%)	10 (38%)	0

Source: Kaiser et. al. 1999. n = 26.

In other words, over half the plans failed to specify clear goals and values, and over three-quarters of the plans failed to provide for effective implementation of their policies and for ongoing monitoring and evaluation to judge whether their programs were working as intended. At least half the plans were a C (average) or worse on every measure. There were also serious lacks in integration of individual plans with overall regional planning. This does not inspire confidence in the CAMA approach to land use planning.

Kaiser and his colleagues acknowledge that CAMA has raised the baseline standard of planning, including water quality issues such as wetland and aquatic environment protection. However, they note that CAMA plans are weak in prescribing goals and strong overarching policies, and they ranked behind non-CAMA plans in specifying future land use patterns. They were particularly dismayed to find lack of attention to capacity, as well as suitability analysis to provide consistent projections and to ensure that future development does not jeopardize the quality of water supply and resources.

To be effective, a land use plan should:

• Analyze the suitability/capacity of land for various uses, including conservation and development. Suitability analysis assesses vulnerability of natural systems (combinations of soil, water, vegetation), capacity of infrastructure (roads, water supply, waste disposal), and patterns of existing land use. Successful examples of suitability/capacity include the plans for Sanibel, Florida, and Lake Tahoe, Nevada.
• Allocate areas for future use based on suitability (supply) and estimated need (demand). This is typically done by using population projections and sizing the future urban areas to be no larger than is necessary to accommodate the projected population for the planning period.
• Direct future development into the areas designated as suitable for it—the urban transition areas on the land use plan, using various growth management techniques, such as zoning, subdivision regulations, and capital improvement programs.
• Coordinate local land use plans and regulations with regional plans and regulations to ensure that natural and man-made systems that cross local boundaries are respected.

Why has the CAMA Promise Not Been Realized?

As a young planner in the 1970s, I was skeptical of the original "go slow" strategy for implementing CAMA planning. However, I was advised that the only way to carry out effective planning for the coast at that time was to use a gradual approach, because of the initial skepticism of coastal local governments about government planning and because the twenty coastal counties were unhappy that they, and not the remaining eighty counties, were singled out for this planning requirement.

The strategy was to first get the local governments to make plans, and then when they are comfortable with planning, get them to implement their plans. Under CAMA, as adopted, local government development regulations only had to be consistent with plans within designated AECs.

But in 1994, 20 years later, when the Coastal Futures Commission reported that the time had come to require plan implementation outside the AECs, there was an outburst of resistance.[vii] The NC County Commissioners Association even passed a resolution demanding that this "unprecedented" intrusion by the state into local land use planning be rejected and disavowed by the governor, Coastal Resources Council, and Coastal Futures Committee.[viii] So much for an incremental implementation strategy!

However, plan effectiveness is not simply a matter of requiring implementation. It also requires that the plans be prepared so as to direct growth into those areas that are most suitable for it and to preserve those ecological systems that are necessary for environmental health. It requires that the plans are consistent with each other and with a regional vision of conserving critical natural resource systems. Finally, it requires that plans be regularly evaluated to see how they are performing relative to adopted sustainability indicators, such as water quality.

What Can Be Done to Achieve A Sustainable Coast?

The Coastal Resources Commission imposed a two-year moratorium on CAMA land use plans in 1998, in order to evaluate the program and make it more effective. To achieve this, the Commission

vii. The North Carolina Coastal Futures Committee recommended that the General Assembly should amend CAMA to require that all local land use ordinances be consistent with locally adopted and approved CAMA plans.
viii. North Carolina Association of County Commissioners. 1994. A Resolution Concerning the Coastal Futures Commission. Adopted 25 August, 1994.

has appointed a seven-member Land Use Plan Technical Review Team to work toward improved CAMA planning. They are working with a facilitator and are scheduled to submit their recommendations by July 2000.

I offer two recommendations for improving North Carolina coastal management. First, re-think land use planning, adding a regional level environmental systems plan and matching the planning requirements more closely with the available planning resources. Second, redesign plan implementa-tion to build in local development regulation consistency fostered by state implementation incentives.

Land use planning needs to be rethought and strengthened. Without a clear and strong overall regional framework, there is no basis for judging the consistency of individual local plans with the state's Coastal Management Plan. The Coastal Resources Commission should map critical environ-mental systems and their connections on a regional scale, and prepare a regional land classification plan that designates primary areas suitable for development and conservation. This regional plan should be based on a solid scientific footing addressed to carrying capacity and it should be coordinated with the river basin plans. It could become the basis for consistency determinations of state, as well as local, actions.

Without adequate resources, local planners cannot conduct the necessary suitability analyses, technical studies, and implementation monitoring for ensuring sustainability. Given budget and time limitations, it stretches available resources too thin to require all 92 separate coastal jurisdictions, large and small, to make detailed plans for the Coastal Resources Commission (CRC) to review. A more realistic and efficient approach would be to focus the CAMA land use planning requirements, as well as the state and local staff resources, at the levels of the twenty coastal counties and the larger cities.

Since all plans are required to be updated every five years, this would mean that the CRC would be able to conduct detailed reviews of some five plans per year, instead of the current average of some eighteen plans per year. More staff time, state funds, and CRC attention could be devoted to these major plans. The remaining minor plans for the smaller communities could be much less detailed and simpler, and could be required to be consistent with the land classifications of their county plans, with differences negotiated through a process of cross-acceptance.

In summary, a more effective approach to land use planning would involve:
• preparing an overall regional plan that is based on a systematic analysis of the carrying

capacity and suitability of the land and natural systems, including analysis of the development inducing impacts of providing access over bridges and highways to fragile environmental areas;

• focusing CRC reviews on the land use plans of the 20 counties and the larger communities, and requiring those major local plans to be consistent with the regional plan;

• ensuring that the designated urban growth areas are closely tailored to projected growth needs and respect the natural systems' functions;

• asking the smaller communities to make less detailed plans, and setting up a cross-acceptance process between the counties and their municipalities to ensure that these minor plans are consistent with the county plans.

Implementation also needs to be strengthened. It makes little sense to prepare a local plan that the local government is going to ignore. Precedent exists in a number of states, including Maryland and Tennessee, for effective growth management in which local zoning is used to implement plans. In Florida, the adopted local plans must include implementing development regulations and capital improvements programs. Unfortunately, in North Carolina there have been court decisions that undermine the relationship between planning and zoning, holding that plans are only advisory.[ix] Thus, it would take an act of the legislature to require this consistency of planning and zoning. In the past, that action has been opposed by the local governments.

In order to make planning and zoning consistency more acceptable, the state could use incentives, such as additional state funding and facilities, for those locations within approved local plans where zoning and other local implementation tools, such as capital improvement programs, are consistent with the plans, and where sustainability measures are met. This type of positive reinforcement for local regulatory and spending actions might help to overcome the unfortunate "you can't make me be consistent" attitude. It has been used successfully in Maryland's Smart Growth Program, which awards state grants for capital facilities to Priority Funding Areas designated by county plans, along with open

ix. According to a January 21, 1999 memo from Robin Smith, Special Deputy Attorney General, to the Coastal Resources Commission, North Carolina state courts have held that local zoning generally need not conform to a master plan. Since state zoning law did not require consistency with a comprehensive land use plan, a specific legislative mandate would have been necessary to impose this requirement on coastal local governments and in adopting CAMA, the legislature chose not to impose that mandate outside the AECs.

space grants to those areas designated for conservation by the counties.

In summary, a more effective approach to implementation would involve:

• adopting implementation strategies as part of the plan, so that the package of plan, regulations, and other implementation tools becomes official policy;

• rewarding consistency of local plans and development regulations, such as zoning and subdivision ordinances, through financial and other state incentives;

• rewarding those local governments whose implementation efforts are successful in meeting environmental sustainability indicators, such as measures of water quality, wetland functioning, and species regeneration, through financial and other incentives.

These may sound like radical proposals. But they are considerably less demanding than many other states require, and they are simply common sense. What we have been doing to plan and manage our invaluable coastal area has degenerated into an unfortunate adversarial relationship between the state and its local governments, with unsustainable results. We need to turn the tide in a positive direction.

Land use planning should be seen as an opportunity for local governments to build consensus about their vision for the future and how to get there, with incentives from the state for doing it well. At the same time, the responsible state agencies should see CAMA as an opportunity to collaborate with local governments in developing a sustainable coastal region. If we don't change the way we manage our coast, it faces a bankrupt and unsustainable future.

David R. Godschalk

David R. Godschalk is Stephen Baxter Professor of City and Regional Planning at the University of North Carolina at Chapel Hill. Godschalk is a Fellow of the American Institute of Certified Planners. He has served on the Board of Directors of the American Planning Association, and been elected to the Chapel Hill Town Council. He has been editor of the Journal of the American Institute of Planners and chair of his university department.

His degrees include a B.A. from Dartmouth College, a B.A. in Architecture from the University of Florida, and a Master's and Doctorate in Planning from the University of North Carolina. His practical experience includes serving as vice president of a planning consulting firm in Tampa, as planning director for Gainesville, Florida, and as consultant to state and local governments in Florida, North Carolina, and New Jersey, as well as in Portugal and Saudi Arabia. He has taught planning at Florida State University and the University of Hawaii.

His current research and publications focus on land use and growth management, natural hazard mitigation, and public dispute resolution. His research has been supported by grants from the National Science Foundation, the U.S. Department of Housing and Urban Development, the U.S. Office of Ocean and Coastal Management, the Lincoln Institute of Land Policy, IBM, and the N.C. Division of Coastal Management.

If you would like to correspond with any of our contributors regarding their essay, please do so via our website,
www.coastalcarolinapress.org

2 8/03